Creating Pastures

A PLAN FOR KINGDOM LEGACY FOR THE CHURCH AND FAMILY

CREATING PASTURES
A Plan for Kingdom Legacy for the Church and Family

Copyright © 2022 Kim W. and Valerie K. Brown

Published by Spirit Filled Creations LLC
Chesapeake, Virginia 23323
www.SpiritFilledCreations.com
Email: SpiritFilledCreations7@gmail.com

Unless otherwise indicated, all Scripture quotations are taken from the Holy Bible, New Living Translation, copyright © 1996. Used by permission of Tyndale House Publishers, Inc., Wheaton, Illinois 60189. All rights reserved.

Cover Design: Spirit Filled Creations LLC

International Standard Book Number: 978-1-7342948-5-9

First Edition
Printed in the United States of America

Contents

Dedication

My entire spiritual life needs to be dedicated to so many people who have helped shape my growth mindset and got me where I am today. So, I'll begin my dedication by honoring four men of God who've impacted my life the most.

My biological father, John W. Brown, taught me how to serve a congregation when I was a child. He embodied caring for the sheep while serving as pastor of Shiloh Missionary Baptist Church in Boykins, Virginia. As a teenager, Pastor Joe B. Fleming became my pastor and showed me the value of developing ministry staff and the need to be community focused. The late Bishop Eddie L. Long impacted my theological precepts, challenged the religion in me, and provided the framework for understanding Kingdom leadership within the church structure. Finally, Apostle I.V. Hilliard taught me the value of family in ministry, operating by faith, and maintaining integrity. As I operate today, I can see characteristics of each of these men of God within myself. I am indebted to God for loving me enough to allow these mighty men to help shape and impact me.

Finally, I dedicate this book to my wife, Valerie. As demonstrated throughout this book, you will see how Valerie serves as a significant part of my story. She has supported, stretched and influenced me as I developed a closer relationship with God. Elder, as we affectionately call her, has been and continues to be my source of wisdom and consistency. She is my sounding board, pusher, encourager, and the perfect helpmeet for me to accomplish all that I have achieved to date and in the future, by the grace and favor of God. When I say, "God made Valerie, especially for me," I'm not exaggerating. She is strong where I am weak. I love her dearly and my life wouldn't be as pleasurable without her by my side.

Foreword

Creating Pastures: A Plan for Kingdom Legacy for the Church and Family serves as a wisdom guide rather than a set formula and is an accurate way to describe Bishop Kim and Elder Valerie Brown's ministry experiences. While many perceive them as an overnight success, they see themselves as daily learners, thirty-plus years in the making. Together, they are open-minded to receive enormous instruction on how the church should function in ministry and how they should function within it as cutting-edge leaders.

Contrary to what many believe, Bishop and Elder did not begin their ministry journey with expectations of becoming a megachurch. Bishop says, "Let us tell you about the entire journey because I think people think that this (megachurch status) is what we were pursuing thirty years ago. No, we weren't pursuing this. While I may not have been happy teaching Bible study to three people, I can honestly say megachurches were not even prevalent at that time. The most one could hope and pray for was a church that could support a full-time salary for the pastor and perhaps a full-time secretary."

Bishop Brown's focus then and now is to serve people faithfully.

Within these pages chronicling their journey are several examples of how divine intervention pushed Bishop to rely on his ability to listen and trust God's process. Without patience, perseverance, and innovation, The Mount Global Fellowship of Churches would not have the influence and impact it has today. While many pastors want the quick success of this fellowship or are looking for cookie-cutter steps they can follow, the reality is they do not want to endure the sacrifices and challenges that qualify them for it. Early on, Bishop recounts a pivotal conversation, "When I came to Mount Lebanon, my pastor, Joe Fleming, told me, 'Son, if the preacher will visit the sick, the sick will come to hear the pastor preach.' It took me some time to understand what he was saying, but when he finally unpacked it, he said, 'When you go over there, please know you're not going over there as the pastor. You are a preacher right now, but if you serve people well, you will become their pastor.' Little did I know that this would be the first principle I learned in how to grow our congregation: love and serve the people, don't lord it over them."

The consistent culture of integrity, excellence, and teamwork associated with The Mount brand directly results from Bishop and Elder Brown's rigorous spiritual growth and dedication to the Lord's leading.

Bishop and Elder are amazed by His grace, and as you turn each page of this book, I extend a personal invitation to join them on a beautiful spirit-filled journey.

Monique Jewell Anderson
Best Selling Author
Author of *Plum Crazzzy, Karma, and Removing the Fear*
Owner of Spirit Filled Creations LLC Publishing

Introduction

I once heard that legacy means "putting a stamp on the future and making a contribution to future generations." I define legacy as something handed down by a predecessor. I believe all of us leave a legacy when we die. The question is, what kind of legacy will be left for others? Do we deposit a legacy of debt and bad decisions, or one that propels the next generation forward?

I live next to a fully functional horse ranch. I have 200 horses as my neighbors, and I am always intrigued to watch the care of maintaining their pastures. I have learned that there are different types of pastures. Some are for grazing, exercise, and others are for growing hay. This knowledge has helped shape my convictions on having a plan to *create pastures*. As a part of my legacy to my family and the church I have been blessed to lead, I have created a plan that feeds them (grazing), exercises them (their gifts, skills, and abilities), and provides an environment in which they can grow (growing hay). While other pastors and I often work diligently to create pastures for kingdom legacy in the ministry, we often neglect to create pastures for our children and family.

It becomes the responsibility of those who fully understand legacy to prepare the next generation for Kingdom ministry and service and Kingdom family legacy. Nothing embarrasses the Kingdom like a believer driving expensive vehicles not paid off and living in mansions with a huge mortgage but dying with no life insurance or inheritance. Yet, the Bible clarifies that God expects us to leave a legacy for our children and their children (Proverbs 13:22). In fact, each generation should feel compelled to take the meaning of legacy to new levels.

Creating Pastures: A Plan for Kingdom Legacy for the Church and Family is my attempt to share with you my journey of successes and failures in the hopes that it creates a pathway for my family and the kingdom to follow and begin to create their pastures.

PART I

Kingdom Legacy
For The Church

Chapter 1

The Early Years

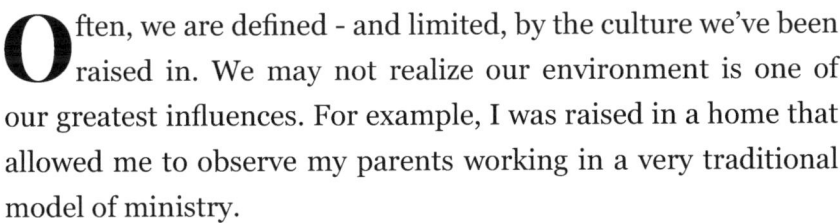

Often, we are defined - and limited, by the culture we've been raised in. We may not realize our environment is one of our greatest influences. For example, I was raised in a home that allowed me to observe my parents working in a very traditional model of ministry.

Growing up the son of a Baptist pastor, I'm quite familiar with every church tradition and personal sacrifices pastors make. Like how my father served at Shiloh Baptist; it was an hour drive away from our home, yet he'd get up early Sunday mornings in time to stop at a hospital in South Hampton County to visit sick members. Witnessing his commitment shaped much of my theological ideologies and taught me the importance of serving and developing a strong work ethic.

My mother was president of the beautification club, responsible for church aesthetics. She would donn the largest, most extravagant hat to church on Sundays without fail because that was the church's expectation for First Ladies. As I spied her from my seat on the front row in my double-breasted suit (looking like a junior deacon), even I was in awe of her elegance. Our Sunday best became a ritual of sorts and provided the perfect cover as I learned how to *do church.* I may have been young, but I was a quick-quick study to do church.

My mother was the perfect instructor because she was an expert at it. If you grew up in church you know that smoking in secret ran rampant throughout the Baptist church as it was considered a cardinal sin. My mother, however, plowed through two packs a day. As soon as the car door closed on our way to Shiloh, she lit up and puffed until the church sign came into view.

At a young age, I was taught the art of the double standard.

As the last cloud of smoke disappeared, my mother tossed the pack into the glove compartment, then sprayed a load of Binaca in her mouth to cover the stench the cigarettes left behind. We then pulled ourselves together to resemble the family whose smiling faces were plastered on the back of the church fans, hopped out, and strolled across the parking lot. I felt fake as we scurried inside the building, posing as a perfect, polished family but hiding behind the stones we silently cast at imperfect members of the congregation. At a young age, I was taught the art of the double standard. The family who lived in our home was never the same as those who showed up for church.

I am not implying that I was traumatized in the church or that my parents were monsters. On the contrary, I have fond recollections of climbing the bell tower at Shiloh to observe the trustees counting the offering and eating leftover communion bread that the deaconesses had freshly baked on First Sundays. During the revival, I had the privilege to stay at the home of a deacon and his family, while my parents stayed at the home of another. Even the bishop that came to guest preach the entire week was a lesson in how the saints love a shepherd who serves with compassion and grace. It was exciting to see how a little rural church in Boykins, Virginia transformed into one of the leading churches in the county under my father's leadership.

Now back to my family...

We sold the entire First Family visage with class and almost award-worthy performances as parishioners eagerly sopped it up. On Sunday, we were revered; the rest of the week, our household was filled with hell.

Religion dictated my every move. If it wasn't ritual or tradition, I wasn't part of it. I was forbidden to play Trouble or any other board games using dice

> **Religion dictated my every move.**

because my pastor-dad didn't allow it. Oh, it didn't stop there, either. Old Maid and Go Fish was nixed because playing with cards was worse than dice; they didn't want me gambling. Going to the movies was a rare occasion, especially on a Sunday, and countless other activities were banned that I was devastated to be excluded from. Keeping up appearances became more of a ministry in our family than actually witnessing with our true lives.

Doing anything appearing to buck Baptist rules wasn't going down as long as it was in front of someone else, but once we were home alone, anything went.

Even more amazing to me was that we weren't allowed to do the same things the deacons, trustees, and other church leaders did. Why weren't they held to the same standards we were? Didn't we all call ourselves Christians? It seemed so cruel. That unnecessary baggage was why I ran away from my calling for so long. There was no way I would serve an institution that had stolen my family and robbed me of my childhood. I'd be crazy to give up my adulthood to the church as well. While my father was a tremendous leader, there were (and still are) days when I felt robbed of the time we could've spent together. He should've been at my ball games, taken me fishing, or do something to spend time with me outside of church—just me and him. Instead, I wasn't having fun like normal fathers and sons. Those things may seem so minuscule to others, but it's hard being on the receiving end of missing out on them. It's even harder not to resent it.

However, when my parents divorced when I was 12, my entire world was obliterated.

As much as my parents tried sheltering me from it, their attempts to hide their volatile relationship failed miserably. They were too busy wounding each other to cover me, so I learned to self-medicate with ministry. It was my escape; I learned to successfully put on a show and do church to survive. However, when my parents divorced when I was 12, my entire world was obliterated. No longer the pastor's son but just a regular church member, we joined Third Baptist Church in Portsmouth, Virginia. To this day, I have no idea what ripped my parents apart; they never attempted to sit down with me to clarify or explain. Without that closure that I crave, I've been left to put together bits and pieces of information to try and make sense of the pain.

For many years, I harbored anger about my childhood, vehemently blaming ministry for robbing me of the memories normal children experienced. I was helplessly caught between two worlds that I considered good and evil. Even my school pictures showed when my life changed. From first grade until junior high, I was the reflection of a junior preacher, with my side-parted hair, dry-cleaned suits, and neckties. I grew my hair into an afro post divorce, dropped the suit, and tried my hardest to convey thug life. My parents hadn't just divorced – I divorced their religious expectations too. There will be no more killing myself to live up to the church's strict expectations of a preacher's kid and trying to be pure and perfect. I finally enjoyed being a *regular kid*, doing things I'd never done before. I was finally free.

Don't get me wrong because I felt strongly about my convictions. However, just as there were many positive

> **To this day, I intentionally remind myself that being in ministry doesn't mean sacrificing family.**

lessons learned from that season, there were also negatives. To this day, I intentionally remind myself that being in ministry doesn't mean sacrificing family.

Many pastors sacrifice family time for the sake of the ministry; however, as an adult, I've understood that the *family* was created in Genesis while the church was birthed in Acts. I often reiterate to the congregation I oversee that the family is the first institution created by God. Pastors - please know it was never God's intent for the family to take a second seat to ministry. We have equated ministry with God in error. Our love for God is always first; ministry is what we do to serve Him. Therefore, if we love God, we will honor His institution of the family.

Through extensive self-reflection and by the power of the Holy Spirit, I've been able to work into a place of wholeness. However, I've also opened my eyes to the fact that the beginning of my marriage was wrought with complications because of the unresolved issues my parents' divorce left behind. This is discussed in greater detail in my book, *Marriage Talk*.

It wasn't until I was called to ministry that I realized how the religious culture I'd been raised in adversely affected my mindset. Before you judge my family too quickly, please understand that my parents only passed down what they'd been taught to me. Growing up in ministry can be one of the most rewarding experiences, but it can also lead to insecurity and warped perspectives if not properly balanced. Too often, we waste our efforts on becoming who people desire us to be rather than concentrating on whom God has called us to be. Authenticity is one of the greatest expressions of self awareness; pleasing God should always override pleasing people.

My childhood experiences served as the foundation for much of my theological and spiritual beliefs, from watching my mother leading auxiliaries to witnessing my father forsaking us in favor of his pastoral duties. I was trained to work in the church at all costs. There's never been a time when I wasn't actively participating in church life. I'm proud of my spiritual foundation, but I readily admit that it didn't help me reconcile my relationship with the church. I knew how to work in the church but was completely oblivious to how to allow the church to work in me.

I believe our work in the church defines our relationship with Christ because that's what I was taught. I did my part, driving the church van, singing in multiple choirs, operating the video cameras, and volunteering in the drama ministry. Yet, as much work as I did to prove I was a *good Christian*, I was woefully barren. Something was missing. Many believers think working and serving in church defines their relationship with Christ-like I did. While serving the Kingdom is important, it's not a substitute for developing a deeper personal relationship with God. Kingdom service should result from our relationship with Christ, not its example.

The last time I saw my father alive was as he lay dying. I was 17.

That day, I fought through my unresolved anger to drum up the strength to make it to the hospital. Yet, years of regret, resentment, and confusion dripped from my pores as I entered his room. I was shrouded in unanswered questions and desperate for a resolution I wasn't prepared to receive. A combination of sadness and anger nauseated me, but I had to see him. Apprehensive yet hopeful that I would emerge a changed man, I looked into my father's eyes and extended both of us the grace we needed to overcome our painful past.

Instead of the volatile confrontation I anticipated, my father quietly received me. It was awkward at first, but I pushed through. He even spoke a word of prophecy over me regarding my calling. Instead of fighting with me, my father used a portion of his last breaths to urge me to submit to the destiny God had planned for me. I failed to understand that my father passed his mantle of ministry on to me in the middle of his room, opening my eyes to one of the greatest blessings of my spiritual journey. My father solidified relationships in our community with men of God who would later become mentors and models for me: Pastors O.L. Cromwell Sr., Ronnie Joyner Sr., and many others whom I intensely studied as I surrendered to embrace the call.

Aside from my parent's divorce and my father's death, two significant events impacted me in my youth. First, the pastor of Third Baptist Church died, and Pastor Joe B. Fleming was appointed to succeed him. God allowed me to develop a relationship with Pastor Fleming, which was critical in developing my call. Secondly, I was crushed when my mother was diagnosed with a brain tumor. I'd already lost my father. Now I was facing losing my mother, too. As irrational as it may seem, the devastation led me to mourn her while she was living. But that's the space I was in. I was lost, sad, and frightful. Out of options to cope, I waited in the MCV Medical Center in Richmond as she was prepped for surgery. I finally confronted what I'd been avoiding for so long, I acknowledged my call to ministry.

As my mother was rolled into surgery, I promised God that if He saved her, I would preach. Less than an hour later, the surgeon came out to inform my brother and me that the tumor couldn't be found, and the surgery was canceled. You read the words correctly, *disappeared.*

I hear You, God.

In an instant, God's desire to have a personal relationship with us overtook me.

After the doctors reported the wonderful news, I raced back to Portsmouth to meet with Pastor Fleming. I was anxious to tell him I'd been called to preach. However, I wasn't ready for Pastor Fleming's response to what I'd boldly proclaimed.

"If I was going to be a doctor, what would I do?" Pastor Fleming sternly asked.

"Well, you'd go to medical school," I answered the obvious, unsure where the dialogue was headed.

"And if I was planning to be a lawyer, what would I do?"

"You'd enroll in law school, of course."

My excitement was deflating. I just confided that God called me to preach; shouldn't Pastor Fleming have been just as excited for me as I was?

"If you want to become a licensed minister, you're going to have to enroll in seminary."

There was no way I was doing that. No. Just...no. After all, my father was a pastor; he knew what he was doing and taught me all I needed to know about theology and pastoring. That should've been enough for me to get in the pulpit, right? Who needed seminary when I had on-the-job training?

I knew how to preach. For years, I'd been inundated with requests to speak during men's and youth day services for various churches of different denominations. I was a bootlegged preacher if you will. So, when I considered the time, effort, and money it would take to complete seminary, I refused to take on those burdens. However, pastor Fleming was adamant that I was going to school and stayed on me until I grudgingly agreed to enroll. Once I agreed, Pastor Fleming allowed me to preach my first sermon and, to my surprise, asked the church to sow toward my seminary tuition. Praise be to God because the congregation sowed into me the first-year tuition of seminary.

God strategically allowed me to experience ministry from two perspectives, which equipped me to fulfill my destiny as a pastor. I've experienced church from the lens of the pastor to the lens of the laity. And I appreciate the burden of ministry while recognizing the blessing of family.

My Wife

Six months after my first sermon, I was invited to preach at New Oak Grove Baptist Church, where O. L. Cromwell II was pastor. He was the son of my father's best friend and my Godfather, O.L. Cromwell, Sr. I was nervous beyond measure, but that service proved to be a divine encounter that altered the course of my life and ministry. Why? Because it was the second time, I ran into Valerie Johnson, Pastor Cromwell's sister-in-law. I had met her the day before, shopping in a mall while I was out with some of my friends. We were all single male ministers on the prowl for single women. I usually just tagged along and let them do the talking, but when I saw Valerie, something was different. I had to be the one to introduce myself. It was a quick hello and good-bye with no exchange of phone numbers. So to see her the next day sitting next to the first lady, I knew this had to be divine intervention. I knew I had to get her number, take her to dinner-anything to get to know her.

I'd been asking God to send me a wife. But not just any wife. I wanted a wife who understood ministry and what it took to be married to a minister. She needed to balance ministry expectations with marriage, know how to prioritize, and be able to enjoy life. I was determined not to make the mistakes I'd been exposed to in my past. Whoever I married was going to be dedicated to ministry, but we were going to LIVE. Boy, did God answer my prayer.

Six months later, Valerie and I were married.

Keep in mind within a year, I acknowledged my call to the ministry, preached my first sermon, and got married. Little did I know, this was only the beginning of a whirlwind that went beyond anything I could have ever imagined.

A few months later, I was invited to minister at a small church near our home. As it turns out, Valerie had grown up in the area, so when I arrived, I was amazed to see how many members of the congregation knew her. It was 1990; I'd been invited because the church didn't have a pastor; however, before the service began, the deacons made sure I knew I wasn't being considered for the office. A congregational vote had already been scheduled, and it was too late for me to toss my hat in the ring.

I still find it funny when I tell this part of the story because many young people have never seen an answering machine. However, those who are a little older can remember relying on those machines when we missed a call because we didn't have cell phones. A week after that service, we arrived home to a flurry of messages. One message, in particular, left us speechless.

Deacon Albert Alexander informed me that Mount Lebanon Missionary Baptist Church had suspended the pastoral vote and offered me a short trial as interim pastor before rescheduling the vote.

I never applied for the position.

Isn't God amazing? After only preaching there once, I was suddenly in the running to become the next pastor. I'd like to tell you that I preached an incredible, God-inspired message that day. The truth is, I preached a sermon Dr. John Kinney helped us with in seminary at Virginia Union. Ninety days later, I was named the 12th pastor of Mount Lebanon, affirmed by a vote of 33-to-11 in thirty minutes. There were approximately 75 members on the church roster, 44 of whom cast their votes at the meeting. The numbers didn't necessarily matter, though. Not when God had already assigned us to Mount Lebanon.

Even today, I am amazed by how God orders our steps. It's been over thirty years, but the providence of God remains evident in our marriage and ministry. The most remarkable part is that I'd known my wife's sister for years but had never met Valerie until the encounter at the mall and the next day at the church. God's timing is impeccable; His ways are pre-ordained for our good. As the old folks testify, He might not come when you want Him, but He is always on time.

God brought Valerie into my life just as my ministry journey began. Little did I know, our relationship would challenge, compliment, and convict me to become the leader I am today. Having vastly different backgrounds from their mates may intimidate some people, but our differences worked in our favor. Although both raised as Baptists, the way we were brought up in the church was light-years apart, which caused our opposing perspectives on how families are to operate in ministry to collide. My wife challenged my views on everything from our ministry roles to why we operated in certain ways. And I challenged her right back.

Like most pastors, I dreamed of pastoring full-time without having to work a secular job to support my family. Determined to see this dream come true, I attempted to transition from small Mount Lebanon to larger ministries at least four times over the next several years. In the meantime, I worked for the Norfolk Naval Base as I waited for something bigger to come through. I was diligent in my pursuit, but God blocked it each time I tried stepping out.

While I loved pastoring Mount Lebanon, our small congregation couldn't provide a full-time compensation package. Juggling my job with ministry while Valerie worked two jobs was daunting; however, God honored our faithfulness and eventually rewarded me with working at the church full-time. It would be ten more years before Valerie would be added to the payroll, although she worked diligently in ministry as a full-time volunteer. But before we received greater responsibilities, we had to prove we were faithful over the little we already had.

The tremendous blessing of being called to Mount Lebanon was the congregation's patience in allowing me space to find myself as a leader. I'm eternally thankful for their tolerance as I wrestled with discovering who I was and navigating my way through the learning curve. Man, I was also blessed to have an incredible wife who was prepared to take the journey with me. We started together with the guidance of fantastic mentors and role models along the way.

I will be transparent here: Upon becoming a pastor, I operated by the model I learned as a child, which nearly derailed my marriage. This is the stuff pastors don't readily share. Vacations were planned around the National Baptist Conference and revivals. I was working another full-time job, and it was wearing me out. I spent weekends on the road ministering while my family was home mourning my absence. Once I returned from my excursions, the tension in our home could be sliced with a machete. Ministry duties were complicating our life; the entire existence of our family unit hedged on it. Unaffected, I even had the nerve to make my family feel like they should be grateful for the little bit of time I gave them. Basically, I told them to get over it because I had to feed the sheep while they were treated to crumbs. After all, she was supposed to understand that ministry comes first. I saw myself becoming my father, whom I had sworn I would never become, as it related to prioritizing the family at the bottom of the list.

How do you think that went over?

What happened to me as a child hadn't altered the way I balanced ministry with family; however, today, I'm well aware that being a husband and father is a call from God in itself. I may have previously been oblivious to it, but eventually, I was able to see how my first ministry was my family. I had to spend quality time nurturing and developing them and the church.

I almost lost my family because I was married to ministry. My big dreams got in the way of learning the proper balance between both, but I'm so grateful I learned. Unfortunately, not everyone is that lucky. The Body of Christ boasts an extremely high divorce rate, especially among leadership, because we are too focused on what's happening in God's house, oblivious to what's happening in our own. Often, our time is misallocated to the church house, making our priorities go against the will of God.

We may be partners in ministry now, but that's certainly not how my wife and I began. Initially, I refused to accept her as my partner in its truest form, which was called into question as soon as we arrived at the extremely traditional Mount Lebanon.

When I was ordained as pastor, as expected, Valerie began serving as a deaconess. Soon after assuming our new roles, a meeting was called by the ministry leader to clarify the role of deaconess. Of course, all I knew about it was what I'd seen growing up. I casually responded that deaconesses basically did whatever the deacons instructed them to do, like preparing the Lord's Supper once a month. Dissatisfied with my blanket explanation, the meeting ended without the answers the women were seeking, and I was left scratching my head.

Part of the shepherd's responsibility is to help the parishioners' unrest within reason. So, I made it a point to investigate the true intentions of the meeting since no one seemed happy with how it ended. Digging deeper, I discovered the source: one deaconess was concerned about not being equal with the deacons in our church society. The unhappy deaconess in question was Valerie. It turns out God was calling her for a larger role in ministry, but without a model, I was grasping for a way to have her tangibly working by my side. Honestly, I struggled to accept that God was calling a woman into leadership.

> **Honestly, I struggled to accept that God was calling a woman into leadership.**

I'm ashamed to admit that everyone could see the call on my wife except me. It wasn't that I couldn't see it; I failed to reconcile my wife's calling with the ministry model I'd chosen for her – which strayed from God's plans. Behind the scenes, Valerie was already working and walking in her calling. A CPA with her practice, she prepared the church's financial statements, bank reconciliations, and payroll and took on other responsibilities I was fully aware that she was doing. She also gave me sage advice that often proved on point and assisted multiple churches in our region and the nation set up their accounting systems. Valerie tirelessly prepared loan documents established checks and balances and facilitated workshops to help us get on the right financial track. She even taught Bible Study moments, led leadership workshops, and preached Sunday morning worship services. Despite my resistance, she was already putting in the work, although I denied her the title and public authority.

The first of many confirmations to publicly acknowledge her call into the ministry and affirm Valerie into leadership came rushing like a mighty wind during a Sunday morning worship experience. Don't get me wrong – although we were birthed in tradition, our church has always been a very charismatic fellowship. But, on this particular day, the Spirit of God swept through the service, and I noticed something that was so out of character for Valerie. She rushed to the altar during worship, where she had a divine encounter with God.

Anyone who knows Valerie can confirm she's not a woman of pretense or performance. When I saw her lying at the altar, I knew it was real. God used this unfamiliar, extraordinary move to help me recognize the amazing call on my wife and the gift from God she is for the Kingdom and our church. Pretenses can be easily brushed aside, but the anointing on my wife could not be denied.

It was time.

As soon as we got home, I couldn't wait to ask Valerie about her experience at the altar. But, almost immediately, my excitement was deflated when I realized she wasn't as eager to share the details as much as I wanted to hear them. Before this Kairos moment, we had had several disagreements about her being called to ministry and whether I should license her. So, when it came time to tell me what God showed her at the altar, she was apprehensive, and rightfully so.

Let's get one thing clear: I never questioned Valerie's love for God, her ability to deliver His Word, or her maturity in Christ. But, again, she'd already ministered during several services and Bible studies in my absence. It was jarring because I'd never seen a pastor's wife preach before. Valerie wasn't loud and didn't hoop when she ministered. She preferred teaching Bible study and leading workshops/teaching moments instead of preaching Sunday morning services. I wasn't against women in ministry; I had licensed other women who had ministered less than her. It's just that Valerie was my wife, and a husband and wife leading together was almost impossible for me to fathom. After all, I didn't have a reference to model it after.

> **It's just that Valerie was my wife, and a husband and wife leading together was almost impossible for me to fathom.**

Despite her initial misgivings, on the day of Valerie's altar encounter, she took a deep breath and explained that God had admonished her to stop arguing with me about getting licensed.

"Haven't you preached on a Sunday morning without a license?" she said God told her. "Haven't you been facilitating workshops across several states, and national conferences, without a license? So why are you concerned about a license? Just do what I tell you to do and stop worrying about a man laying hands on you and publicly affirming you. I have called and affirmed you, not a man. So just do what I tell you to do, and all will be well."

What could I say after that?

That revelation ended our disputes. I stopped bringing up her preaching style and how she taught instead of hooping. We simply did not talk about the topic of when she'd be licensed. Valerie clearly heard and responded to what God told her to do and went on about doing His business and fulfilling her purpose. She understood that if I never recognized her gift of administration and released her into ministry, she still heard from God. He called her in spite of what I attempted to block. God prepared her to be used in the Kingdom and instructed her to stop waiting for me or any other man (flesh) to acknowledge her call. So she prepared in silence and continued doing the work.

In the Baptist church, any minister who isn't licensed isn't fully respected in leadership and ministry. To embrace my wife's calling, I had to shake many of the sacred traditions I was raised to believe. God was moving. Who was I to try to impede it? It was intimidating, but I was excited to see that God was up to something much bigger than I could comprehend or explain. My wife was being called into ministry formally and possessed gifts vital to our church's destiny. This transition would later prove to be the catalyst that propelled The Mount into levels of ministry that were beyond our wildest expectations.

The final confirmation about Valerie came to me in a dream.

I dreamed Valerie followed a prominent bishop and took notes as she listened to orders and gave suggestions as if she worked for his church. I snapped from my slumber and woke Valerie up, asking if that bishop had offered her a job because if she were going to work for any church or pastor, it would be me. Through this dream, God compelled me to empower my wife. He was telling me in no uncertain terms that Valerie had gifts to be used in the Kingdom, and if I refused to employ her as both her husband and pastor, He'd ensure someone would.

Remember, no one knew Valerie was doing this work except for myself and the financial secretary on The Mount's payroll. As a CPA holding a doctorate in business management from Case Western University, Valerie was more than qualified for a paid position. Still, she went unpaid, unrecognized, and unappreciated for ten years. It takes a strong woman to brush pride aside and serve in humility the way Valerie did. She remained quiet and stayed consistent in her commitment to supporting the church and me. She's truly one of a kind; I don't know of one wife who possesses the skills Valerie does, who would've been content taking a backseat for so long. This is why God has redeemed, elevated, and blessed Valerie tremendously for her obedience to His voice.

I'm happy I finally listened, too.

Chapter 2

Understanding Kingdom Versus Religion

My upbringing caused me to be extremely comfortable when I was called to pastor The Mount, a traditional Baptist Church. God had already groomed me for the position: my uncles were pastors, and my Godfather was, too. Moreover, Baptist pastoring was in my blood. From as early as I can remember, I spoke at youth programs, sang lead in the choir, and spent most of my time at church. Coming into pastoring, I was more equipped than the average young man; I'd already been given the wings to fly.

For over thirty years, I've pastored one church. All these years later, I'm grateful for those who saw something special in me and gave me a chance to truly learn how to be a shepherd. Several Mount partners were members when I arrived and remain to this day. Those are the ones who helped develop me. I'm eternally thankful for their commitment to my family and me, but more importantly, their faith that God called me to lead them.

When I arrived at The Mount, growth was slow. I was in seminary at Virginia Union, sitting under great theologians yet becoming more confused about church leadership and what ministry should encompass. Going in, I thought I knew church. But, come to find out, what I knew was how *to do church.*

I was the Sunday school commentator for the local branch of the Baptist Ministers' Association, which gave me visibility among the well-known pastors of larger congregations in our area. The exposure I gained from that assignment garnered me more preaching engagements. I found myself preaching numerous revivals around the state, dragging the church choir along with me to some interesting places. Yet, as busy as I was, I felt a void. There had to be more to church than what I was experiencing. Then, Valerie began diving deeper into the Word and challenged my perspective on Baptist polity in the most uncomfortable ways. It forced me to earnestly seek answers to clear my confusion. As a result, I consulted God for deeper ministry perspectives instead of opinions.

As a result, I consulted God for deeper ministry perspectives instead of opinions.

One day while in a Christian bookstore, I spotted *Charisma Magazine.* As I waited to check out, I picked up the magazine, flipped through the pages, and stumbled upon an ad for a conference. It was hosted by New Birth Missionary Baptist Church in Atlanta, where the late Bishop Eddie L. Long was senior pastor. I was urgently compelled to attend. However, I didn't know why. That single decision catapulted me into my destiny in drastic ways, and I wouldn't trade it for anything.

Immediately, I began researching New Birth and Bishop Long. I felt God pushing me deeper into understanding my role in the Kingdom, and I thirsted for more of His presence. Initially, I was intrigued by New Birth's transition from a traditional Baptist church to a ministry with a Kingdom mindset and leadership model. The Baptist church had not embraced the Office of the Bishop. Yet there I was, getting acquainted with a bishop at the helm of a major Baptist church. I wanted to explore this new thinking, as well as megachurches that were on the rise. The largest church I'd known maxed out at 1,000 members in its heyday. Though I'd dreamt of pastoring a larger congregation myself, I hadn't imagined anything bigger than that.

Confused and intimated, I was so hungry for mentoring that I regularly called New Birth, trying to reach Bishop Long. Calling and calling to no avail, I refused to be deterred or give up. Finally, one day this sweet church mother, who must've been a volunteer, answered what seemed like my thousandth call. As I had so many times before, I asked to speak with Bishop Long, expecting to be rejected again. Now keep in mind that I wasn't aware there were thousands on the church roster, but this sweet mother educated me that day. She informed me I needed to call Bishop's office to set up a meeting and to be prepared to get in line for a date. Then she asked where I was from, to which I informed her I was from Virginia. Even today, her advice to me is crystal clear: "Young man, if you believe God wants you to meet Bishop, then you need to go to the church where he's ministering next Friday...in Virginia. God will make way for you to meet and speak with him."

Scrambling to know where Bishop Long was preaching, I was delighted to find he was headed to Norfolk to consecrate Pastor B. Courtney McBath as a bishop. I couldn't wait to meet and witness his ministry in person. I am still overjoyed that Valerie and I pressed our way to the service; what a celebration it was. Never had I seen such apostolic order - it was like being in Kingdom university. The experience was phenomenal; it ignited the Kingdom mentality I hold onto today. This man I'd only seen in a magazine was right in front of me, and I couldn't believe it. I will never forget it.

Beginning with the processional, to say that God was moving was an understatement. Before that evening, I'd never participated in such apostolic grandeur. So let's start with the line of people wrapped around the building, waiting to get inside when we arrived. Valerie and I just knew we wouldn't make it in, let alone find a seat. But God.

Thankfully, an usher recognized us. We were escorted inside the building and into the waiting room with a slew of other pastors to line up for the processional. As we waited, we were informed that we would proceed into the sanctuary in apostolic order, where seats were reserved for us. I refused to display my ignorance, but I didn't even know what apostolic order was. I still laugh about how God orchestrated the moment.

As we lined up behind the bishops, apostles, elders, and presiding elders, I felt like the very least and the last—*just a pastor*. I felt so small and insignificant, like I didn't belong. But then, just when I thought I couldn't feel any lower, the scripture I'd studied so often came alive within me: "The first shall be last, and last shall be first" (Mathew 20:16).

I still don't understand how Valerie and I sat front row center after being at the very back of the line. In awe of our sudden favor, I heard some of the clergies seated behind us asking how we scored such incredible seats as if we were attending a sporting event. It didn't matter if they wanted us there or not; Valerie and I were right where God wanted us to be. Peace washed over me. I didn't respond, keeping my mouth closed and my heart and mind wide open.

As the evening unfolded, I was like a sponge, soaking in the music, prayers, processes, protocols, and the commanding atmosphere. The entire time there, the sound of the sweet mother's voice admonishing me from New Birth rang in my ears. I was so happy I listened to her. If I hadn't, I might have lost out on my destiny.

Admirers swarmed Bishop Long at the end of service, but God nudged me to walk on the platform and introduce myself to him. When I told Valerie I planned to approach Bishop, she nodded to the security team, standing guard like they were waiting for someone to get out of order so that they could bounce them out of the sanctuary. As intimidating as the situation was, I was confident in making the connection happen.

I've always been a stickler for order and typically not bold enough to hop on the platform the way I did. Still, God granted me a different type of courage that night. After all, there was a church mother in Atlanta praying for me. This was a divinely manifested opportunity I was determined not to miss. So, faith leading the way, I braced myself, whispered a prayer, and then darted into the pulpit. However, before I could tap Bishop Long on the back, he turned around and greeted me first. That brief encounter was truly a turning point in ministry for me.

Without flinching, Bishop Long informed me that God told him while he was ministering, he was assigned to mentor me and that I was his spiritual son. I was astonished; I wasn't going to have to do the work alone. It all seemed surreal, but the mother I'd spoken to hinted that this meeting was ordained. Even today, when I drive past Calvary Revival Church, I remember how God plucked me from tradition and catapulted me into His Kingdom mandate during that service.

My first visit to New Birth was beyond anything I'd ever experienced. It was all gloriously overwhelming, from the parking lot ministry to the greeters, the television cameras, the world-renowned choir, and the people packed in the crowded pews. The presence of God was so strong that Valerie and I remained in the sanctuary an hour after worship ended. The custodian was attempting to lock up the building, and there we were, sitting in the back, overcome with emotion and processing what we'd just experienced. God was up to something big, and we didn't want to miss anything.

On the way back to the hotel, neither of us could stop talking about service. The Spirit of God alone kept us finishing each other's

> **No, what we beheld was a life-altering encounter with the divine.**

sentences and chatting nonstop. There was no way we could return home without introducing the experience we'd been a part of to our congregation. It wasn't to be written off as a convention where you get pelted with sermon after sermon, then solidify your preaching calendar for the year or a vacation disguised as ministry. No, what we beheld was a life-altering encounter with the divine. All I could think about was, "hold on, this is going to be a ride."

There were so many commonalities between New Birth and Mount Lebanon. Both were the Missionary Baptist denomination and had a history of leadership struggles. Exposing me to New Birth was as if God gave me a glimpse into my future if I opened my heart past religion and tradition.

Fully recharged and ready to soar into my new beginning, I spent time listening to tapes of Bishop Long's teachings and traveling to Atlanta as much as possible to sit under great men and women of God for wisdom impartation. God introduced me to Dr. Sam Chand, whom He'd later use to instill grassroots changes at Mount Lebanon.

God performed a dramatic overhaul on almost every area of my ministry.

God performed a dramatic overhaul on almost every area of my ministry. All I could do was cling to my basic Biblical foundations as every area of my theological beliefs and perspectives were radically shredded. As much as I wanted to remain steadfast on what I believed, I knew God was giving me crucial revelations about church - or better said, religion.

Like peeling the layers back from an onion, God began transforming Valerie and me and Mount Lebanon. The more God revealed, the more I was forced to rethink my vision of the gospel truth. After a while, I realized that many of my ideologies weren't rooted in the Bible. I'd been functioning in man-made traditions (denominations) Mark 7: 6,7 (NLT).

As I searched further for the truth, I braced myself for an epic battle between religion and Kingdom. But unfortunately, the tension between these two realities is unrelenting. Every day, the congregation could see the changes in Valerie and me, and I fervently prayed they could handle this new pastor God was developing.

As I became more Kingdom-minded, the small church God had entrusted to my stewardship began to grow; however, we were still deeply entrenched in Baptist traditions. Our basic leadership model placed authority on the joint board, comprised of deacons and church trustees. Biblically, deacons are called to assist the pastor in serving the congregation. At The Mount, the deacons and trustees held authority over the pastor. They were also responsible for annually evaluating the pastor and determining his compensation. No vision could be shared with the congregation by me without first consulting with the joint board for their approval. If the board disagreed with the vision, it was blocked.

The Mount's governing documents were the constitution and bylaws, which stated decisions were to be sent to the joint board for review before proceeding to the congregation to vote on and ratify. As I became more Kingdom-minded, my leadership style shifted. My excitement and efforts to lead the church into a Kingdom model intensified. As a result, tension grew between the board, which exploded during one of our monthly meetings, and me.

Before the meeting, I had no idea a letter had been circulated declaring I was to be confronted about leading contrary to The Mount's constitution. My future as pastor would be decided by the members that night. Valerie had always told me that every leader is eventually confronted with a defining moment in their tenure, but who knew that time had come for me. I pulled onto the unusually crowded parking lot, expecting the worst. I knew something was up but was clueless that I was the center of controversy.

All thirteen concerns were valid and accurate – I had been leading outside of my written authority.

During the meeting, concerns were raised about how my leadership style conflicted with the church constitution. All thirteen concerns were valid and accurate – I had been leading outside of my written authority. However, although they meant well, the board had previously stifled my vision. As a result, I often approached the congregation directly without consulting them. I gained the members full support of my vision, which became the source of contention between the board and me, along with other conflicts.

None of the concerns about me were moral or ethical; they were all based on procedure. Control, if you will. I had to sit in that meeting as each of the board's concerns was meticulously checked off one by one, like a grocery list. As bad as I wanted to make excuses to clear my name, Valerie advised me not to give them any. I humbly accepted the accusations being hurled at me, confirming the congregation was right to be concerned. I was not leading by the constitution/bylaws.

I'm not sure how long it took to reach the end of their list of grievances, but when they finally did, I was relieved. As I exhaled, trying to control my composure and maintain some semblance of professionalism, a new partner of The Mount unexpectedly took a stand for me. He said he had no problem with me or my decisions or how I was leading the church and that it was clear this was a leadership issue between the board. He noted that all the new members had joined because they enjoyed my relatable leadership style. He made a motion granting me the power to rewrite the constitution to line up with my vision and operational processes. A second to the motion quickly came, and the congregation overwhelmingly approved it.

In an instant, God transitioned our church from the traditional model that man orchestrated to a reflection of His Kingdom. Though not everyone agreed and made the transition with us, the vast majority of the congregation understood God was in the midst of the changes, clearing a path for the church constitution to be rewritten to line up with the vision I presented to them.

Overnight, almost every area of our church exploded like wildfire. Our structure became more apostolic, and I was given the authority to make decisions

> **We all just needed time to adapt to the new regime.**

without approval from the board. The chain of command pivoted; however, I didn't usurp their ability to assist me in leadership because their support was vital to our success. We all just needed time to adapt to the new regime.

Keeping the board involved wasn't a requirement; however, I was transparent with them, which was vital to building confidence moving forward. Making crucial decisions without seeking the wisdom and counsel of the elders is dangerous. Working together, we were able to implement strategies to impact our community and fulfill our call from God. It wasn't easy - there were numerous stumbling blocks along the way, such as the collisions between the previous and new models. Despite the challenges, I'm proud to say the saints of The Mount were strong enough in the faith to be guided by the hand of God.

Every time I was discouraged, God sent us to New Birth to be refilled by people who motivated us to stay the course and embrace the process. Our maturing season was stressful, but it was necessary. This is why I'm a strong advocate for pastoral coverings. Every pastor needs a pastor who motivates, encourages, and inspires them to become what God has ordained them to be. When the legacy of Mount Lebanon Missionary Baptist Church is recorded, the influence of New Birth Missionary Baptist Church will be an integral part of her history.

Chapter 3

Understanding the Office of the Bishop and Pastoral Covering

My aunt was a mother in the Church of God in Christ who introduced me to the Office of the Bishop at a very young age. In Southeast Virginia, we were extremely proud that some of the most prolific bishops in the Pentecostal movement pastored in our region. These men were the epitome of leadership and entrepreneurship and were a source of great influence to many.

As Baptists, we weren't concerned about reverencing bishops, so I sought the direction of the Holy Spirit to see how bishops fit into the Baptist setting. My research produced some very practical results.

In the last few years, the title and Office of the Bishop have been manipulated and misused to the point that many have shied away from it. In fact, its blatant misuse has caused some formidable

> **I've noticed many pastors functioning in the office respond to *the call* yet don't officially acknowledge the title itself because of the concerns it causes in some circles.**

pastors concern over formally accepting the title of bishop. I've noticed many pastors functioning in the office respond to the call yet don't officially acknowledge the title itself because of the concerns it causes in some circles.

The body of Christ is severely undereducated on what the Office of the Bishop truly means and entails. This has led to confusion among Believers that the church has yet to recover from. Aside from that, the behavior and lifestyle of some bishops (and, unfortunately, many pastors as well) have caused a lack of respect for both offices. As a result of this negative atmosphere, many pastors have sadly declared, "If that's what a bishop is, I don't want to be called one."

One of the major roles of the Office of the Bishop is to educate, inform, and teach the Biblical principles of apostolic authority with credibility and accountability. In addition, our roles should help the Kingdom reclaim the respect of the Body of Christ and provide the needed leadership for this dispensation of time. Simply put, bishops are the gatekeepers who accept the charge to restore biblical offices and maintain Kingdom structure, accountability, and order.

In the midst of a rapid growth spurt in our church, we shifted our perspective from membership to partnership, believing as partners, we believe in divine exchange. During this time, a slew of pastors requested that I act as their spiritual covering. Partners of our congregation began calling me Bishop, and The Mount planted its first church. I was uncomfortable being informally granted the title of bishop when I hadn't been able to reconcile the Baptist church's failure to recognize it theologically. I refused to embrace it myself and attempted to continue walking in Baptist ignorance. This isn't to be taken as disrespect toward the Baptist denomination. Every denomination has gotten some standards correct, while others are theological opinions and not necessarily biblical.

Despite my resistance, partners of the congregation accepted the Office of the Bishop before I did, pushing me toward a better understanding of apostolic order and development for our church's continued evolution.

Even with the support from The Mount, pastors submitting to my leadership, and friends who were bishops, my Baptist roots continued to get in the way. However, I couldn't deny that God was moving in my life, revealing the truth along the way.

> **I discovered that I'd allowed my denomination to become the source of my understanding instead of the Holy Spirit.**

As He led me to build relationships with other Kingdom-minded leaders, many blanks in my confusion were filled. I discovered that I'd allowed my denomination to become the source of my understanding instead of the Holy Spirit. This needed to be rectified.

Now along with everything else going on around this time, I happened to be perusing a copy of the National Baptist Church

Hymnal when the Holy Spirit led me to the *Baptist Articles of Faith* in the back of the hymnal. Many churches may still do this, but every traditional Baptist church member remembers reading the church covenant inside the front cover of the hymnal during communion on first Sundays. That same book has the Baptist Articles of Faith printed in the back, proving the adage somewhat true: *If you desire to hide something from African American people, put it in a book.* Apparently, a majority of African Americans don't read - including the Bible that Christians profess to believe. But that's a topic for another day.

It was time for me to learn for myself. Reading the Articles of Faith, I was shocked to see verbiage I'd never seen before. Article 13 reads:

"ARTICLE XIII. A Gospel Church.

We believe the Scriptures teach that a visible church of Christ is a congregation of baptized believers, associated by covenant in faith and fellowship of the gospel: observing the ordinances of Christ; governed by His laws; and exercising the gifts, rights, and privileges invested in them by His Word; that its only scriptural officers are bishops or pastors, and deacons, whose qualifications, claims and duties are defined in the Epistles to Timothy and Titus."

Can you believe it? Right there, in the back of the book, the articles clearly state that the Baptist church only upholds two biblical offices of leadership: the deacon and the office of pastor and bishop. How could this have been in the hymn book all this time without me knowing it was there? In my research, I'd never even asked if the title of bishop was biblical. Instead, I asked if it was Baptist. Not to mention, if bishops are recognized in the Baptist Articles of Faith, why do so many Baptist churches refuse to recognize the Office of the Bishop?

> **Not to mention, if bishops are recognized in the Baptist Articles of Faith, why do so many Baptist churches refuse to recognize the Office of the Bishop?**

After discovering the Baptist denomination did not recognize its own Articles of Faith regarding the Office of the Bishop, I understood God was purging me of religious rhetoric and elevating my thinking to prepare me for a new season of grace in Kingdom leadership. That said, I was still perplexed about the difference between pastors and bishops and if there was even a difference. Suddenly, it seemed as if bishops were springing up overnight. Please let me make it clear that I'm not attempting to discredit or disagree with anyone else's beliefs, but I want to clarify our ministry's perspective on apostolic order and where my resistance stemmed from.

The good and the bad of denominational autonomy is the ability of each church to shape its theological point of view. Even with opposing theological perspectives on various topics, I've learned that everyone doesn't have to agree on every precept in order to walk together, as long as we agree on our basic tenets of faith. This is where the line between pastors and bishops becomes blurred. Not only was I struggling to figure it out, but the congregation was approaching me with the same questions I had. Unfortunately, it didn't seem like I was any closer to finding the answers for any of us.

"What is the difference between a bishop and a pastor," some wanted to know. "What are the qualifications of a bishop?" Others inquired. "Is every pastor a bishop?"

I wanted to know, too.

The questions pummeled me faster than I could get answers, so I examined a slew of bishops, thinking it would help resolve the confusion once and for all. Guess what? I was worse off. Why? Because across the board, there were inconsistencies in what qualified anyone to be called a bishop. I won't argue the definition of pastor versus bishop; however, church partners see pastors lead the church, preach, and teach on Sundays and Wednesdays, and care for the congregation. Then they see the pastor one day declare himself a *bishop* the next without any change in function; it can become jarring to partners. This is where things get complicated.

I wasn't going to take the title of bishop without first understanding what it meant.

I wasn't going to take the title of bishop without first understanding what it meant. The wonderful thing was that I studied the Bible for myself. As a result, I came to several conclusions, along with the guidance and wisdom of seasoned, Christ-filled leaders and the Holy Spirit.

First, the Office of the Bishop and pastor are related but not identical. To differentiate between the two, The Mount and our Council of Elders agreed that in the context of our ministry, I would teach that pastors are shepherds (leaders) to sheep (partners), and bishops are shepherds (leaders) to pastors (leaders). Pastors are sheep before becoming shepherds and revert to sheep after the season of pastoring ends. To that extent, every pastor needs a bishop.

The bishop manages and holds you accountable while your pastor cares for and serves you. I can honestly say that if it weren't for strong bishops holding me

> **The bishop manages and holds you accountable while your pastor cares for and serves you.**

accountable for my integrity, character, and lifestyle, counseling and disciplining me on my transition from sheep to pastor to bishop, I wouldn't be the leader I am today.

Aside from the disparities I've already mentioned regarding the Office of the Bishop, I would like to enlighten you on the process it takes to become one. Again, I am not attempting to disqualify the legitimacy of anyone who calls themselves a bishop; I'm simply seizing the opportunity to express my theological perspective.

As a bishop myself, it's concerning that the Baptist church has failed to create a structured process to become a Bishop, let alone a pastor. In fact, many people declare themselves bishops with no formalities at all. A great metaphor the Body of Christ uses to identify the Kingdom is *the army of the Lord,* which is also expressed in the Bible. In the natural army, we don't become generals without a process of matriculation. The military would think we're crazy if we just wake up one day calling ourselves a general; it doesn't legitimately happen overnight. It takes years of experience, mentoring, and promotions to be elevated from soldier to general. On the flip side, in the spiritual, Bishops are the same as Generals in the natural.

Based on protocols I gleaned from Bishop Long and Bishop I.V. Hilliard, I've been personally convicted about the qualifications of becoming a bishop in the church. Let's start with numbers, which convey structure and revelation in the Bible. Biblically, the number twelve represents established government and authority. For example, twelve distinct and distinguished disciples walked consistently with Jesus. As children, we sang songs about the twelve gates to the city. Then there were twelve tribes in covenant together that became Israel.

Based upon this, it's my practice to only consecrate to the episcopacy pastors who have at least twelve sons and daughters or cover at least twelve churches and have pastored without moral failure (and other established and written guidelines) for at least twelve years. While this may appear to be stringent, I would argue that we've become too relaxed. I am proud of the bishops I have consecrated because I operated in confidence based on the evident fruit in their lives and ministry. The size of the ministry or the number of partners in the church is never my criteria. I don't judge the tree by its size, but rather by its fruit.

Not only should we be concerned about the qualifications for consecrating bishops, but also employ the witness of others as qualifiers. Matthew 18:20 states that where two or three are gathered in God's name, He will be in the midst. 2 Corinthians 13:1 reminds us that out of the mouth of two or three witnesses shall every word be established. And finally, 1 Timothy 5:19 reminds us never to receive an accusation against an elder without two or three witnesses.

When Bishop Long prepared to consecrate me, he required that I have at least three witnesses communicate their support of my consecration in writing. Mirroring that standard, I have become committed to maintaining a standard of witness.

The Bible uses two or three witnesses as the standard; therefore, The Mount requires two or three witnesses to prepare written statements and verbal declarations at the consecration, testifying the individual's worthiness to be elevated to bishop based on their fruit. The first witness is from the candidate's leadership, the second is from ecclesiastical colleagues, and the third hails from the community in which the pastor serves. When Bishop

Long consecrated me, it was meaningful to observe civic leaders, the mayor, and various pastors who comprised the credible roster of witnesses who supported my elevation. Every pastor needs support. But did you catch this as you read my testimony: The pastor who didn't believe bishops belonged in the Baptist church was, in fact, being consecrated a Bishop. And as part of the consecration council were Bishop Eddie L. Long, Bishop Eric Garnes, and Bishop Copeland. All are highly respected and recognized Bishops in the College of Bishops. Only God! The Year was 2010.

Pastoral Accountability

To reiterate, one of the biggest challenges within the body of Christ is the lack of pastoral accountability.

Every profession sets performance parameters. For example, no one is licensed to be a doctor without graduating from medical school and passing written and practical medical boards; annual reviews and continuing education requirements must be met to maintain eligibility. Then there are teachers who must meet educational requirements, pass written and oral exams, and continue their education to keep their positions. Lawyers are required to pass an exam and have continuing education. CPAs must pass an exam and then have continuing education. See where I'm going here? A *license* is a public affirmation that a governing body oversees your credentials and ensures that you stay current to do what the license has granted you permission to do.

To work in a specific profession, proper protocol and certifications must be met - except in ministry. This isn't to say attending seminary is the deal breaker to becoming a minister; however, there should be a standard and universal education to assume the position. This isn't difficult for me, seeing as how I've always been a life-long learner. Over the last thirty years, I've matured in ministry because I've been opened to continuing education, both formally and informally, through mentorship. This openness had catapulted me so much further than where I was when I began. Who wants to employ the services of a doctor or lawyer who hasn't stayed abreast of the latest technology or refreshed their skills since they were first licensed? The Body of Christ should require no less.

The church is the only institution where we can slap a title on ourselves and start a ministry without anyone questioning or challenging our authority to do so. Microwave ministries' timeline looks like this: get saved in August, licensed by September, start a church in October, and call yourself a bishop when November comes. No real standards are being upheld, and that's why the church has lost a massive amount of the respect it once held in the community. So, whose shoulders does it fall on to restore the trust that has been broken? The bishop.

> **The church is the only institution where we can slap a title on ourselves and start a ministry without anyone questioning or challenging our authority to do so.**

So often, we hear 1 Timothy 3:1 quoted by the saints: "He that desires the Office of the Bishop desires a good work." But unfortunately, the word desire has become a strident source of misguided theology. The office of pastor is a calling; no one should deem himself a pastor any more than being allowed to crown himself a bishop. Ministry is not the same as clocking in and out of a corporate job; once we respond to the call of God, we're on duty 24/7.

It's all right to want to be a bishop, but it takes more than a desire to help the office regain its lost credibility in the Body of Christ. One of the most important parts of 1 Timothy 3 that is often overlooked is the fact that bishops also desire a *good work*. Being a bishop is much more difficult than being a pastor; pastoring sheep is easier than pastoring shepherds. Shepherds require a totally different level of needs and concerns.

> **Bishops are also accountable for the lifestyle of those in ministry and for protecting the church's doctrinal foundation.**

Bishops are also accountable for the lifestyle of those in ministry and for protecting the church's doctrinal foundation. The Bishop or Council of Bishops is tasked with disciplining pastors or church leaders who have fallen victim to immorality, teaching false doctrine, or indiscretion.

In the traditional Baptist church, pastors are accountable to the deacons. In sharp contrast, accountability is always provided by higher-ranking officers in the army. Biblically, deacons are to serve as assistants to the pastor; therefore, they cannot or shouldn't be allowed to discipline pastors who technically rank higher than them. Pastors should answer to bishops, but in the absence of accountability, deacons have stepped up in their place. This is an erroneous misstep in the Baptist church. The pastor is often recognized as an employee who works for the deacons and the people, eclipsing their authority when leading the church.

Earlier, I mentioned my leadership challenge; however, I want to expound more to emphasize a different view of accountability.

In 1996 as the church gravitated toward a more apostolic structure, it never occurred to me that based on the church constitution, I was out of order. I thought the Holy Spirit was guiding me, but I overlooked the constitution and Book of Roberts Rules of Order as the authority on church protocol, policies, and procedures. In many churches, leaders refer to these guides more often than the Bible.

As the church grew and giving increased, at first, all seemed well. Remember the letter I mentioned citing the 13 infractions I'd committed against the church constitution? Again, the packed parking lot that night was a sign that something was amiss. Most folks don't come to church to conduct business sensibly; they come to argue. The success of the black church is found in its roots of liberation in America and is the first institution where freed slaves had authority. Out of the black church sprang most of our legacy universities. Moreover, because of the way the black church was birthed, it also met the craving for social gatherings and organizations in their community. This created a challenging dynamic for the pastor to effectively lead because of the conflict between who were the leaders: the deacons and trustees or the pastor?

The night of the meeting, the partners flexed their power to prove where my authority began and ended. It's worth pointing out that not long before this occurred, the men of our congregation had journeyed to The Million Man March in Washington. A guest who attended with us had recently joined The Mount and showed up for this church meeting. After a heated deliberation concerning the letter, the new partner abruptly stood up and said, "I actually joined the church because I like the way Pastor Brown is leading. It seems the problem is between the leadership and not the partners." This statement solidified my belief that the real power is in the pew, not the board. Hence, we to this day are congregationally ruled by the people and not by a board. As if that wasn't enough, he concluded his statement with a motion that I be given the liberty to rewrite the constitution to line up with my vision to alleviate conflict and bring our structure into full constitutional compliance.

After he took a stand, another new partner enthusiastically seconded the motion. In the end, the congregation voted to grant me the authority to redact our church constitution and by-laws. A moment that could've been very divisive in the life of our church had become the catalyst to propel us into one of the most impactful churches in our region.

After the meeting, I returned home, humbled that God had trusted me enough to grant me that kind of authority.

> **I'm proud of The Mount's integrity.**

I'd been given much and would be required to establish proper channels of accountability to steward the confidence the partners had in me. To date, I'm proud of The Mount's integrity. Too many times, pastors take advantage of their position and lead with a weak structure. They're not held accountable to anyone and refuse to listen and share the leadership with others whom God has gifted with the capacity to assist them.

While I have the apostolic authority as a bishop, our church has developed a tremendous team with shared governance that maintains integrity and accountability while upholding me as a visionary. Together, we have established confidence and a clear understanding of the biblical roles of the church officers. As such, we have been able to accomplish so much for the Kingdom of God.

Guarding The Doctrine
——— ..

All scripture is inspired by the Holy Spirit and is good for teaching, rebuking, correcting, and training in righteousness, according to 2 Timothy. Whenever the gospel is manipulated, it becomes the responsibility of the bishop to correct the fallacies or manipulation of the doctrine. Bishops are guardians of sound doctrine, which pales beneath unilateral autonomy in the Body of Christ.

The Body of Christ would be much more effective with established systems to hold ministry leaders accountable.

While serving as a chair of the hospital authority in our city, it was impressive to sit at the board table every month, hearing reports from the chief medical officer as they disciplined and monitored the behavior of the other staffers. They hold each other accountable and regulate education requirements and discipline as they restore each other. The Body of Christ would be much more effective with established systems to hold ministry leaders accountable. Guarding the tenants of our faith is crucial to maintaining credible doctrinal stances and developing mechanisms for maintaining the standards of the Word of God.

Pastoral Covering
——— ..

The term covering was initially foreign to me; however, Pastor Tim, a local pastor, was the first to request a meeting with me and ask if I would become his pastoral covering. Many pastors followed then and still continue seeking me out as their mentor, spiritual father, and covering. This birthed my desire to impart into these pastors' lives tangibly. Chartering new territory, I was forced to wrestle with theological precepts considered sacred cows in my spiritual development. I wasn't completely lost; however, there were many models of covering for me to learn and glean from.

Many coverings are as simple as fellowships, while others are considered reformations. Fellowships are opportunities for general relationship building with planned moments of instruction. At the same time, reformations are subject to structure, hierarchy, and doctrine. As I studied the methodology of each, the biggest area of need that continuously resurfaced was *accountability*. This prompted me to research other denominations and the Bible for a better understanding of what a covering is. My studies revealed that the Body of Christ was seriously lacking pastoral accountability. During years of ministry, I have been connected to several fellowships and have had two coverings. My first covering was under the late Bishop Eddie L. Long called The Father's House and currently under Apostle I. V. Hilliard, called AIM (Association of Independent Ministries). Each fellowship covering (although different in what they offered) has afforded me the opportunity to glean both near and far what I have needed to become a better husband, father, and pastor.

Kingdom Keepers

Developing pastors and guarding the faith of the Lord's church are the great priorities of a bishop and should not be slighted. After much research, meditation with God, and counseling from elder statesmen that I respected, God finally allowed us to establish a ministry named *Kingdom Keepers*. Again, because the Baptist church has historically wrestled with pastoral accountability, what it should look like, and who should hold whom accountable, Kingdom Keepers' first objective was to structure a process for leadership accountability in writing.

The second objective of Kingdom Keepers was to minister to the marriages of the pastors. Too many ministry marriages are strained, stressed, and broken. The divorce rate in the pulpit is as high as the divorce rate overall. Pastor's wives are hurting and longing for attention, identity, and need to be ministered to themselves. Many are driven to a lonely place, feeling abandoned by their husbands and the church. Kingdom Keepers was committed to serving those needs. In addition, we saw far too many times pastors' kids neglected and feeling the pressure that other preachers' kids can only understand. We were determined not to lose them like I was almost lost.

Finally, pastors needed assistance growing and developing ministries, so Kingdom Keepers also targeted those areas.

Accountability, family, ministry, and church development became Kingdom Keepers' four-pronged focus. Monthly meetings and quarterly training were the vehicles employed to achieve our overall goals. God blessed Kingdom Keepers to grow into a vibrant ministry, providing a platform for developing numerous pastors across the nation. As the fellowship grew, it became evident that all the pastors were at different levels of their ministry development and required different needs. This became increasingly difficult to custom fit the needs of each pastor within the fellowship along with all my other responsibilities to The Mount. So we decided to establish several levels within the fellowship.

First, there were mentees. For them, I was available to dispense counseling and advice; however, the pastoral role was fulfilled by someone other than me. Next, those who desired a more inclusive relationship were defined as sons and daughters who received wisdom, counsel, and pastoring. This was a much more definitive relationship, with apostolic leadership covering the sons and daughters we served.

As Kingdom Keepers continued to soar, it became increasingly difficult to distinguish relationships from one another because many pastors began to share that they wanted and needed the relationship to be more than what was offered to the group. This brought confusion between the pastors and me and the pastors within the covering themselves.

Due to the number of conflicts, I grew frustrated with the idea of covering pastors and sought direction from God about the future of Kingdom Keepers. Although we felt we identified and articulated what Kingdom Keepers was, was not, and what it offered to pastors, we realized many of them needed more than what we could offer them consistently, which left me with some tough decisions to make.

I inadvertently operated Kingdom Keepers like a church by welcoming anyone who desired to join. But unfortunately, this whosoever will approach provided a platform without a covenant relationship and solid commitment. Pastors wanted access to the platform's influence but wanted no part of accountability. Simply put, I had an abundance of spiritual sons and daughters and had fallen into the trap of measuring success by numbers. Just as pastors view the impact and success of their ministry by how many people are in the pew on Sunday, I gauged Kingdom Keepers' success by the number of pastors on the jam-packed roster.

"If you have so many sons and daughters, why are there so many of them who don't look like you?" She asked.

Valerie told me not to toil over the numbers because God wasn't concerned about them like I was. To her, I should have been focused on quality. It seemed so simple, but her observation was theologically insightful. "If you have so many sons and daughters, why are there so many of them who don't look like you?" She asked.

When they see my natural children, people assume, "You look like Bishop Brown's child," because the resemblance is striking. Yet, mentally scanning the roster of pastors who'd joined Kingdom Keepers, it was evident that many of my spiritual children didn't resemble me at all. Not that I wanted clones, but I wanted to see pastors who displayed my character, ethics, integrity, family values, and desire for Kingdom churches. It was disheartening to see how much that was lacking in the organization I founded and led.

Jesus poured everything into 12 disciples. While His following far surpassed the twelve, the multitude didn't come close to having the intimacy He did with them. Kingdom Keepers was dissolved after much personal reflection and seeing how ineffective our large roster was. I'm not criticizing other organizations, as each has its purpose. Still, Kingdom Keepers wasn't conducive to my calling and how God desired me to serve other pastors. I can be more intentional with a smaller group of pastors who hunger for more than a large group. Time is one of the most valuable resources we have. I desire to spend mine sharing the lessons I've learned, developing those I am assigned to, and impacting the Kingdom of God by creating a leadership legacy.

Destiny Circle

Kingdom Keepers was dismantled, and Destiny Circle was created in its place. Much smaller than Kingdom Keepers, Destiny Circle is comprised of the pastors of The Mount Global Fellowship of Churches, as well as a small group of pastors across the nation. My assignment with Destiny's Circle pastors is for me to be more intentional with leadership legacy than what large fellowships allow.

> **Identifying your capacity and assignment is critical in eliminating frustration and distractions as we serve in ministry.**

Identifying your capacity and assignment is critical in eliminating frustration and distractions as we serve in ministry. Remember, obedience is better than sacrifice (1 Samuel 15:22-23). We do not receive credit for performing work God hasn't assigned us, no matter how great the work is (Mathew 7:22-23). We must be committed to the calling and assignments of God in our lives. We cannot fall victim to using superficial mechanisms as a measure of success. Bigger isn't always better, and numbers can't unilaterally define ministry. Zechariah 4:6 reminds us that God does not operate by power or by might but by His Spirit.

Never allow anyone to make you feel bad when you truly believe you heard from God and act upon that knowledge only to return, regroup, and start again. I don't know if I am actually starting over again, but I know I am clearer about what God is saying to me. I realize I have matured in my understanding of the role of the bishop and what I have to offer to the next generation. As I am in the season of prayer on who my successor will be for The Mount at Chesapeake site and ascend fully to The Office of the Bishop only, I have come to realize that I have more years behind me than ahead of me. This has caused me to become even more intentional about the use of my time and the development of pastors desiring my covering and mentoring. The Destiny Circle of pastors has been very informative and enlightening. I truly believe the pastors have been blessed to have had greater access to me, and their ministries have increasingly benefitted from the knowledge, wisdom, and advice that has been imparted.

However, God is moving me to make one more transition in my journey to understanding what it means to be a Bishop. I believe this new revelation is coming now because I am ready to release The Mount at Chesapeake to my successor. It requires a great demand on my time, and I cannot lead them and move into this next journey of my ministry being fully committed to the work of the Office of the Bishop. God has blessed The Mount Global Fellowship of Churches to currently have nine locations and an event center called The Signet Center. It is a signature event center that includes a banquet/wedding venue, state of the art conference center for breakout sessions, a full gymnasium, a full commercial kitchen for catering, and an eight-lane bowling center with gaming stations, billiard tables, etc., as well as a teen residential care facility. So to fully embrace this next move, I will be releasing the Mount at Chesapeake and have formulated the following covering structure.

The Mount Global Fellowship Of Churches Site Pastors

Under the Destiny Circle model, the Mount Global Fellowship of Churches' pastors has been a part of that covering structure. However, it has become quite clear that the Mount pastors need their separate covering. They have a different level of commitment and investment in the future of The Mount fellowship, and I have a different conviction for their individual growth and development as pastors to ensure their success within the fellowship. Therefore, the Mount pastors will have their retreats, meetings with me, guidance, and advice moving forward. Together we will focus on the future of the fellowship under the divine guidance of the Holy Spirit. There may be times when they meet with other fellowships and coverings; however, they will have what they need specific to their needs and the Mount Kingdom.

Issachar Leadership Circle (ILC)

The Issachar Leadership Circle is still in its drawing board season. This will be an exclusive opportunity for pastors to join a dynamic group of like-minded pastors who desire to be among the leaders in kingdom ministry. This group will be iron sharpening iron and will feature speakers from around the world who are leaders in their own right. This circle is perhaps the final chapter (unless God says something different) of my journey to leave this Earth empty, having poured all thirty-plus years of ministry experiences, successes, lessons learned, and failures into the lives of pastors who want to learn from them.

The greatest joy of a bishop should be pouring himself into the lives of the pastors who have been assigned to him by God. The mark of a bishop isn't in the size of the fellowship or reformation but the evidence (fruit) of the pastors' lives he has positively impacted for the greater good of the Kingdom. My prayer is that I leave a great legacy of fruitful pastors.

> **The greatest joy of a bishop should be pouring himself into the lives of the pastors who have been assigned to him by God.**

Chapter 4

Introduction to Church Planting

I'm often asked how we got started in church planting. I would love to say it resulted from some fantastical epiphany, but the truth is the seed was planted on a Sunday afternoon drive home from church.

At that point, I'd been blessed to pastor The Mount for over 20 years. One of the unexpected blessings I received was the number of associate ministers we had at all experience levels. Some were the children of pastors, new ministers, and former pastors who were no longer pastoring but very gifted. That afternoon, I made a comment to Valerie about how blessed we were to have so many *stallions* joining the fellowship.

I must admit it was quite inspiring and good for the ego to minister on Sundays and see such a proficient group of ministers who felt led to sit at my feet. Did you know that the ego can become a source of failure in ministry if not properly and often checked? However, when I mused over this with my wife, I was taken aback when she casually responded, "You do know stallions aren't meant to be corralled, right? Stallions are meant to run, and preachers get mad when they knock down the fence and run – or in this case, leave and start their own ministry."

Valerie's simple statement, to this date, has led to nine Mount locations and crafted a blueprint for church planting that has proven to be successful and meaningful for the Body of Christ. Before I could offer a rebuttal, she declared, "Why don't you start Creating Pastures in which they can run?"

When we first started planting churches, we purchased two facilities simultaneously. A grocery store was purchased and transformed into our Chesapeake Cathedral location and a furniture store in Elizabeth City, North Carolina. Both stores were renovated into beautiful edifices. I served as the senior pastor for both locations, which taught me one of my first lessons: pastoring two different locations is not as easy as it sounds. Church plants hear all the time, "One church in multiple locations." While this might be theologically and practically true, multiple locations create multiple needs, issues, and concerns. Think about it this way - I was pastoring one church over one hundred years old (Chesapeake), and then we had a baby (Elizabeth City) in our old age. It was a complete culture shock and a shock I wasn't sure I could get used to.

So many times, what we call faith is improper planning or impatience with God's timing to prepare for expansion.

It is important to note that church planting isn't for everyone. The decision to begin planting shouldn't be driven by ego or the desire to become a larger church. It should be a direct mandate from God and recognized as a Kingdom assignment. Unfortunately, too many churches begin planting without counting the cost. Luke 14:28 reads, "But don't begin until you count the cost. For who would begin construction of a building without first calculating the cost to see if there is enough money to finish it." So many times, what we call faith is improper planning or impatience with God's timing to prepare for expansion.

I'd never heard the term *church planting* used in the Baptist church. Unfortunately, most church growth in the Baptist church happened through splits that weren't necessarily amicable. Almost every city has a *First Baptist, Second Baptist*, and a *Third Baptist*. All of them came from the First Baptist, yet they are all still there. Developing an intentional strategy for church planting shouldn't focus on splitting but should be seen as a biblical mandate. The Bible is the greatest manual on church planting. As we developed our principles to plant, we realized that well-thought-out plans and processes pave the way for Kingdom expansion, which enabled us to be more productive in making disciples for Christ.

The purpose of planting churches is birthed out of the foundational purposes for which Christ established the church from the beginning and is the primary vehicle for equipping people to become disciples. Church planting has become much more prevalent in the Western-influenced American church movement in the last decade. Although necessary, church planting should not be driven by a desire to build an empire. I often hear people lament, "We have enough churches." But where are the complaints that we have enough drug stores, retail outlets, grocery stores, or car dealerships? We are selectively choosing industry over Kingdom.

Planting opens the door for diversity in the types of churches that are established in the community, with a well-rounded spattering of spiritual tastes and assignments. No single church can meet all of the spiritual needs of a community, nor should it attempt to. Just as car dealerships sell a plethora of makes and models, churches are equipped to offer various forms of ministry to satisfy the needs of their congregations.

I like to say we are liberal in our methodology yet conservative in our theology.

Before planting a church, ask yourself if the community has a genuine need for the type of ministry you are called to serve. The Mount is a non-traditional Baptist church that believes in operating in the gifts of the Spirit. I like to say we are liberal in our methodology yet conservative in our theology. The needs of the community should be the ultimate catalyst in determining where a church should be planted.

Check your motives: are you erecting a building or making disciples as Christ originally mandated? We aren't just called to make disciples but to baptize, which is well-documented in the Bible. The baptizing component of the Great Commission confirms the need for church planting, according to Matthew 28. In Titus 1:5, the Apostle Paul displays a full strategy for the mandate of church planting. Appoint elders in every town and recognize that the church building is not the church but the people of God. The building is a reminder that the presence of God is there while serving as a haven for those seeking a relationship with Him.

Perhaps another reason for planting new churches is because they tend to be more appealing to young adults. Older, well-established churches have become vested in practices akin to sacred cows. As a result, they aren't as open to new strategies and methodologies to attract the next generation. I'm not talking about changing your beliefs as a Christian; I'm urging you to change your *delivery* of the gospel.

Cell phones are excellent examples of pivoting in ministry to meet people where they are. The convenience of cell phones has influenced most homes to ditch landlines; however, we are still able to communicate effectively. In transportation, we drive cars to get from point A to B, but technology has beefed up the way we get around. The same can be said for the modern church. The basic tenets of our faith are still being taught, but how we spread the gospel has changed.

I consider myself a traditional churchman. As a result of my upbringing, I have a healthy respect for the sacred components of church and worship and try to keep an open mind regarding methodology. However, clinging to the ways of old can stagnate our future. For example, when we were children, orange juice came in a glass jar with a metal cap. Today it's packaged in a plastic jug.

Remember, it is the same product, in updated packaging. If the church is going to continue winning souls to Christ, the church is obligated to be open to new packaging. Same Christ, same gospel repackaged to attract its current audience.

One of my first decisions as pastor of Mount Lebanon was to purchase a drum set for the sanctuary. Well, one of the deacons had a fit, saying, "The Mount is not going to use money to tolerate any of that *bump, bump music* in God's house." Since the deacons weren't open to *repackaging* the worship experience at the expense of the church, the next week, Valerie and I took my honorarium from preaching at a week-long revival and purchased the drums ourselves, without touching The Mount's finances. Before the constitution was rewritten, my hands were seemingly tied to any decision I wanted to make, even one as small as buying an instrument.

When the deacon who'd given me all that grief arrived the morning of service and saw those drums, I thought he would combust. Before service, he convened all the leaders into a meeting. As I walked in, his wrath smacked me in the face. "I thought we told him he couldn't use church funds to buy a drum," he growled.

"But I didn't use any church funds," I defended myself, "I preached a revival at another church and bought them with the compensation they gave me."

I won't go into it here, but this is why pastors need to have their finances to do the work of the Lord when instructed and not simply buy another suit or pair of shoes. But back to the deacon.

"It doesn't matter," the deacon spat, "there's no one here who can play the drums, anyway."

Oh, how wrong he was.

God always has a plan, and I was certain He had one to justify my sacrifice. That Sunday, Mother Edna Brown came to visit with her grandson – Eddie Joe, in tow. And guess what? That Eddie Joe could play the drums to Heaven and back. After playing that day, he was the first drummer to join The Mount. Not only did he join, but God also used Eddie Joe to shift our worship experience. Multiple instruments were implemented to enhance our services; it was a divine elevation. Of course, we continued singing gospel songs of Zion, but those tunes were *repackaged* to appeal to the unchurched and those who'd grown disenchanted with traditional church music.

Inspired by the changes in our music ministry, I began studying the dynamics of worship. As the Spirit of God taught me, the conditions that could affect the atmosphere and effectiveness of the worship experience I'd ignored in the past were revealed. The room temperature, lighting, and sound are vital components that should always be considered to provide the most effective experience possible.

The Bible says our works should be done in the spirit of excellence as unto the Lord. The word *worship* means *to kiss God.* Worship should be seen as an intimate experience, not a service. If the worship center is too cold or too warm, the atmosphere will be impacted. Please note that these tangible components are important, regardless of church size or style of worship.

The Bible teaches us that faith comes by hearing. Today, the church plant isn't measured by the next edifice down the street; it's regarded by the industry standards and technology of the secular world. Why would people pay good money for a ticket to a secular concert with advanced technology and a fantastic sound system yet settle for much less when they come to worship?

I can hear the chatter now from traditionalists who want to justify their failure to adapt by arguing that the church shouldn't look like or copy the world. Please hear me out: we are not changing the gospel; we are improving the package. Presentation is important. Often, the church is seen as a place that compromises excellence, although we represent a mighty, majestic God. If we are His witness, what do the people hear when they encounter us?

Sure, many churches have limited resources and can't afford to invest in high-level technology and equipment, but that shouldn't be an excuse for not doing the best with what we have. Clear sound, a warm facility, and a comfortable space are not major luxuries that are out of reach for the average church. Maybe they cannot purchase an LED screen background, but there is an option to mount television monitors on the wall. Technology has major implications for the growth of a ministry. Without technology being visible in the church, young adults assume the ministry isn't open to new ideas and doesn't embrace change, and eventually fall off.

I'm convinced that growth isn't as important as maintenance to the church in many cases. If the Great Commission is our purpose, the Body of Christ must be open and serious about

– it's the needs of the unchurched that we are trying to attract and disciple.

how the church presents the gospel. As much as I love worship, I always try to remember that it isn't based on my preferences. In fact, if there aren't at least four or five components of your church's worship experience that you could do without, worship will have limited impact and growth. I don't need lighting effects, smoke, or a band to meet my expectations, but it's not my needs that need to be met – it's the needs of the unchurched that we are trying to attract and disciple.

One of the most effective ways to create a fresh worship experience is to engage a creative arts team to evaluate and implement strategies for improving the overall worship expression for the church. This team must study everything from the structure, timing, temperature, music, length of service, sermon presentation, and use of technology. So many times, I hear this method is only suited for large urban churches, but I disagree. A rural church that I assist has effectively facilitated enjoyable worship experiences by incorporating technology and innovation while maintaining a sense of comfort that appeases the seasoned saints and the new generation. The church I observed is experiencing rapid growth and advancing the Kingdom with tremendous success. They've committed to *repackaging* worship and embracing change to become more effective and are committed to spreading the gospel.

Simple technology upgrades can increase a church plant's ability to reach different demographics and effectively lead people to embrace their message and ministry. Never forget that even established religious leaders of the Bible's biggest problem with Jesus was the packaging of His message. It boils down to control. Many pastors shy away from being out-the-box with their message because they know it could potentially impact their authority in the church. Growth can be intimidating; the best way to prevent it is to shackle the ministry to outdated, ineffective processes and strategies. Want to empty the pews quickly? Don't feed the sheep in a manner that they can digest the food.

Sometimes, the greatest holdout to repackaging (or modernizing) the gospel isn't coming from the pews. Resistance is often found directly from the pulpit. I've encountered countless pastors who argue that upgrades are biblical abominations. Pastors often have taken ownership of the ministry they lead in personal and unhealthy ways. Consider this revelation that was shared with me from a covenant son:

"Years ago, our generation was the group God gave new strategies to repackage worship, and we blamed the 'they' (the leadership over us at the time) for stifling our growth and the growth of the church for their failure to embrace these new strategies and change with the times. Now we have become the 'they' as we have gotten older and just like the previous leadership are refusing to listen to the younger generation, move aside or mentor them, and allow them to take their rightful place in leadership."

Now is the time for new strategies to reach this new generation. First, the traditional church must adapt or become extinct. New church plants are many times easier to adapt to change. For example, when I arrived in the early '90s at Mount Lebanon, worship started with the prayer band, deacons leading songs, prayer, and testimony service. I worked diligently to adjust this format to fit what worshippers desired years ago when I was younger, including replacing the choir with praise teams, establishing dance and mime ministries, creating a contemporary atmosphere, reprogramming the music, and implementing new service times, in the hopes it would attract my generation as church attendance and growth had stagnated.

> **Now is the time for new strategies to reach this new generation.**

When I implemented changes at The Mount, I was in my twenties, and I was open to new things. My fearlessness and boldness caused many local pastors to speak against The Mount and me, but I took it all in stride. I was confident in what God told me to do. We were pioneers in our area and being such is never an easy task. Still, somebody has to create the path and be willing to endure the criticism for others to follow. Some of the same people who talked about me have adjusted their worship services because of our example. Did I get angry? I wouldn't call it anger; however, I didn't like the negative talk about me. I have come to accept that it is an honor to be the one who inspires others by succeeding myself.

> **My advice to every pastor is to be open to different concepts and ideas, learn to listen, be prepared to change, and challenge the status quo.**

Change is inevitable and doesn't stop. To that end, it's time for fresh packaging again. We can't be afraid of change or be that generation who holds back the new one because we fear it. Unfortunately, we've become the group we talked about when we were younger. In the wake of God inspiring a new generation to repackage the way we present church, we must acknowledge that our desire to hold onto what we've previously identified as sacred, perhaps God, is attempting to reform. My advice to every pastor is to be open to different concepts and ideas, learn to listen, be prepared to change, and challenge the status quo. Maintaining a commitment to foundational truth and being prepared to shift perspective will help us usher the next generation into even greater realms.

Jesus never repeated the same miracle the same way. He opened eyes repeatedly but differently each time. If the church is to remain relevant, she can't be afraid to try fresh ideas and strategies. God, Himself, reminds us that morning by morning, new mercies we see.

Statistics prove that new church plant's almost always reach the community more effectively than established ones because there is no struggle with leadership over sacred cows and traditions embedded in the old church structure. Therefore, church plants have the opportunity to be more effective in reaching and bridging cultural differences in this new dispensation.

New churches create opportunities for service that are sometimes harder for established churches to break into. In church plants, cliques and lines of authority have not been established. At the same time, old leadership has become engrained in their roles in established churches and fiercely protective of their positions. As a result, it can be difficult for new individuals to find their place in ministry and sacrifice their time and service. There's a reason why the woman breaks open the bottle of perfume at Simon the Lepers' house in Bethany. Much of the time when Jesus visited Bethany, he visited Mary and Martha's house; however, he went to Simon's home this time. This gave the woman an opportunity to release her ministry to Christ. Remember, Mary and Martha's roles were already established at their house. At Simon's home, the roles were not as defined, so the opportunity for fresh ministry was presented.

New ministries develop new gifts and inspire new leadership to discover new people who have been dormant or unidentified. I'm always amazed to see individuals who've been inactive in ministry at one site become a part of the leadership and ministry growth at another location. The opportunity to serve creates commitment. Feeling needed makes us feel more connected. We can't be intimidated by the development of church plants because it has a greater impact for the Kingdom.

Not long ago, I was made aware that one of my partners who'd been with me for years had joined one of our plants. I called her to see what prompted the location change and what I discovered taught me yet another major leadership lesson. She organically embraced my church planting model and reminded me that she'd volunteered in the media ministry when she originally joined our church. As we developed, the media ministry grew with a host of talented individuals. This new level of skills created a higher level of responsibility.

She visited one of our sites closer to her home and discovered they needed volunteers to help start the media ministry. This allowed her to serve and mentor a new generation of media staff. After our fruitful conversation, her response was I would always be her Bishop. She was excited to serve my vision by assisting in the growth of a new site. God sends people for different seasons to help your ministry. For me, this partner's presence created continuity and allowed the main church's DNA to be deposited into the new site. Pastors, please remember that we are under-shepherds; the sheep belong to God and not us.

Pastors, please remember that we are under-shepherds; the sheep belong to God and not us.

New church plants also define the purpose of specific churches more clearly between the co-mission we have in common and a particular mission for that ministry. Just as car dealerships all sell cars but not the same brand of vehicles, we are the Body of Christ. Some churches are hands, others are feet, but we all are called of Christ.

Many feel that church planting has had adverse effects on the survival of existing churches because when a new one opens in the community, people flock to it, even choosing to leave their ministry for a fresh beginning. New plants shine a light on churches stuck in tradition rather than focusing on reaching believers with a different methodology. The new church then becomes an example that the ideas and methods the traditional church refused or was slow to adopt works elsewhere. It's possible that planting a new congregation can energize others that have become too comfortable. The church plant is a Kingdom instrument used to push existing churches into some serious self-examination.

In spite of what traditionalists believe, church planting can build unity instead of creating division. Church plants offer the opportunity for partners to utilize their spiritual gifts, preventing them from leaving if they feel they aren't needed or there isn't room for them to serve. Perhaps this is fueled by a sense of entitlement from existing leaders, or the territorialism often found in ministry. I'm always pleasantly surprised to see people who were passive in the pews at one location aggressively participate in the new one. As the Bible declares, the harvest is truly great, but the laborers are few (Luke 10:2).

Our First Church Plant - Understanding Geographical Culture
—— ··

Our first plant in Elizabeth City, North Carolina (also known as The River City), taught us one of the most difficult lessons we needed to learn in our new venture: Everyone doesn't view church planting from the same perspective. Elizabeth City is a small town located approximately 45 minutes from our main campus. Several pastors with whom I'm associated or consider peers were beginning to plant churches around the same time as The Mount, so, I diligently studied their models, convinced it was time for me to plant a church.

I considered a number of locations in my surrounding area to plant. However, on a weekend drive scouting potential locations, the advice Valerie had given me about stallions came roaring back. And for no apparent reason, we decided to visit Elizabeth City. Valerie had never visited Elizabeth City before, despite our proximity. As we entered through the beautiful waterfront entrance to town, the Spirit of God said this was it – we'd found our home for our first plant.

Disclaimer: Our current planting model has been completely revamped from our previous Elizabeth City plant model, as we will discuss in greater detail later.

Diving in on full faith, there were so many lessons to learn as I assumed the role of senior pastor. I preached two services in Chesapeake, then trekked an hour down the highway to conduct service in Elizabeth City. It was a lot, but I made it work at first.

Please know that when I mention how I made it through the storm, that victory includes Valerie. Our ministry is family-centered, and she was with me every step of the way. For instance, before we had armor bearers to drive us, there were numerous Sundays when Valerie took the wheel as I reviewed my sermon notes. She helped me with Tuesday Bible study in Elizabeth City and then Wednesday night Bible study in Chesapeake. And truthfully, whatever else I needed the rest of the week as I served, visited the sick, counseled, and generally ministered on every level to both congregations. Once we hit our mid to late forties, we realized we couldn't sustain this high energy level for extended periods of time. I was exhausted.

Sustainability is a keyword when contemplating church plants. You have to ask yourself if you can sustain whichever model you plan to execute. It's much easier to start the way you plan on finishing. Lock your model in quickly because changing midstream can prove challenging.

While I realize that the foundation of every church is and should be Christ as the chief cornerstone, the reality is that people connect to a church if they are attracted to their leader's style. I preached multiple services for seven years until one Sunday; my body crashed as I tried to get in a quick nap in the Elizabeth City parking lot. When someone had to wake me up, I knew it was time to stop. Even with the help of armor bearers and Valerie, the balancing act was too grueling to continue any longer. I was depleted.

As the first church I ever planted, I will always have a special place in my heart for Elizabeth City. Serving as their pastor was an incredible experience. However, the mental and physical toil the assignment had taken on me was overwhelming. In hindsight, committing to pastor Elizabeth City was a terrible decision. None of us can predict the future, especially when that future has more expansion through additional sites. Even after God told me my season had ended, I served out of guilt and stuck around because of pride, not the assignment. So, to the detriment of the ministry, I continued serving in disobedience. Nevertheless, the church had grown tremendously. The thrill of reaching the next generation from the local college students migrating to the site kept me behind the pulpit.

With each worship experience, it was exciting to see the multi-generations of worshippers packing the pews. My exhilaration provoked me to conduct multiple three-night crusades, oblivious to how it was deteriorating my mental and physical health. Pride filled my veins like I was hooked to an IV. On Sundays, I was a rock star-hopping from pulpit to pulpit to deliver a Word. Honestly, The Mount was so popular; I loved telling people we were one church in two states. *Beware Pride goeth before the fall.*

Beware Pride goeth before the fall.

Despite the rush of adrenaline I was experiencing, there were two major concerns needing to be addressed in Elizabeth City. First, because I lacked discipline and mismanaged my time, I left the main Chesapeake campus late, leaving the music ministry in North Carolina to serve 50 minutes straight until I arrived. Again, my pride went unchecked, even when it began causing issues at the main campus.

Once I concluded my message in Chesapeake, I'd run out and leave the invitation to discipleship for the associate ministers to handle until it was brought to my attention that if I didn't stay to extend the invitation, the church didn't grow at the same pace. After all, my sudden exit sent a message to potential new partners that I didn't have time for them. This wasn't said off the cuff, but the numbers had been tracked in black and white and spoke volumes. There was no denying that my presence – or lack thereof, made a huge difference.

Another source of contention was a charismatic move of God

on some Sundays at the main Chesapeake campus that made it impossible for me to tear away to make it to the sister site on time. Because of the confusion this was causing, ministry leadership and I planned to have an associate stationed in Elizabeth City to minister if I couldn't make it. While the associate minister was highly qualified to lead service, it wasn't the best strategy because they waited until the last possible moment to make any moves, allowing me every opportunity to walk through the door or notify them I wouldn't be there at all. The congregation got irritated because they expected me to minister, and rightly so. Still, I forged on.

My solution to resolve the issues everyone, including myself, had, was to appoint a site pastor to serve under me at Elizabeth City while I remained senior pastor. Well, as they say, anything with two heads is a monster, which this move proved firsthand. Although the site pastor and I flowed well, it was hard for the partners to adjust to the instability of not understanding who was really in charge. The reality was that he served as pastor Monday through Saturday, and I swooped in as the Sunday morning shepherd. Just being transparent: Afraid of losing partners, I was hesitant to install him as pastor, which would've been the best decision for all of us. The funny thing is, despite my best efforts, many partners fell off, anyway. I was scared of what the congregation thought of me and that I'd let them down; it turns out I still disappointed them.

In one of the most extraordinary lessons in leadership I've been taught in all my years of pastoring, Dr. Sam Chand (a good friend and great advisor to our ministry) convinced me that I created a complicated model that wasn't sustainable (there's that word again) or healthy. Instead of strengthening the ministry, my presence only undercut the site pastor's ability to lead and basically tied his hands. It was time for me to take

> **It was time for me to take responsibility for making things worse because I wasn't mature enough to give up what God didn't want me to have.**

responsibility for making things worse because I wasn't mature enough to give up what God didn't want me to have. "He that desires the Office of the Bishop desires a good work," the scripture says. Tough decisions are work. Making unpopular decisions is work. But instead of working, I was running from the work.

Slowly, I assigned more responsibilities to the site pastor and weened the congregation from me. Finally, I announced that the site pastor was being elevated to lead pastor, and I was assuming the role of Bishop to the partners. I apologized to the congregation and the newly appointed pastor during the lavish installation service for overstaying and operating in pride. It was a wonderful day, yet I wondered if I'd waited too late to make the decision.

My concerns proved to be correct. The pastor did a tremendous job of serving and leading; however, the division I created began to take its toll. I must take full responsibility for several different groups having formed in the church as I drug my feet relinquishing my position. Although disappointed, some were committed to staying on and continued serving with faithfulness. They adjusted to the changes and didn't cause a ruckus. Then others left Elizabeth City and followed me to the main Chesapeake location, ignoring the long drive. I'd been their only pastor for many of them and the relationship between pastor and sheep is incredibly special. I understood why they migrated, but it didn't take away the sting.

Another group of partners didn't make the transition. Understandably, they were upset with me. To this day, I still regret letting them down. I spent many days agonizing and losing sleep over how I negatively impacted many people's relationship with the Kingdom and The Mount. While many parishioners found other places of worship, several disconnected from the Body of Christ. I promised God that if He forgave me for my disobedience, never again would I allow my desires to override His will.

I acted the way I did out of my love of serving God's people (sprinkled with a little too much pride), and it backfired. Ultimately, I'd done everyone a disservice by forgetting the church belongs to Christ, and He can do with her whatever He desires. Christ died for and established her. Pastors are stewards, not owners. It is my eternal hope that those affected will always know my motivation was honorable, even if my methods fell short. My love for the Elizabeth City campus has never wavered; she will always be the first plant baby.

Lessons Learned

Lesson - 1

Wait on God

Five years into serving The Mount, way before planting the NC campus, I was looking for a bigger ministry to go to or start a new one because I desperately was tired of working two full-time jobs. I desired to be full-time in ministry only with a salary to support it. I was also tired of my leadership being called into question (as discussed earlier) and stunted growth. But every time I attempted to pursue something else, it wouldn't manifest, probably because it was out of God's will. God is in control. Sounds crazy, right? Of the numerous attempts I made to leave The Mount, one stands out the most. I was a finalist in the search for a new pastor at a church in our area. The night before, I was scheduled to be interviewed by the church leaders, Valerie and I drove up there and parked in front of the building. I thought, *what an opportunity this would be to serve in ministry full-time and lead a much larger congregation.*

As we sat in front of the large edifice, I asked God for a sign. Don't judge me, but I literally said aloud, "Lord, if this is where we should be, please give us a sign." Before I finished praying, a man ran into the street and began shooting. Bang, bang, bang, the shots rang out. Valerie turned to me and declared, "The Lord spoke quickly, didn't He?" I called the church the next day and withdrew my name from consideration. Several times after that, I had committees from other churches visiting The Mount to check me out as a potential candidate, but none resulted in the open door that I desperately craved. Looking back, I can see that this was all God's doing.

You can't really interview with other ministries without your congregation finding out what you're up to. There's no way around it. Well, word got out that I was a pastoral candidate for other churches, and The Mount wasn't happy. The frowns on the congregation's faces as I preached made it hard to look at them. Here I was letting them down again, but I wanted this so bad. As much as I wanted a job at a new church, every sermon I preached to secure the position ended in disappointment. It was time for me to make it happen. After all, the older folk always told me that if I take one step, God will make two. I was about to take my step.

I decided the best way to make my move was to launch an early morning worship service. I hired a talented musician, developed a praise team, and announced a start date, anticipating it would quickly explode and pave the way for me to start a new church within my current traditional church. I even named it: Kingdom Christian Center. Unfortunately, I had no real theological reason for the name or the ministry; I was just tired of serving without seeing the level of growth I desired. Sadly, it was all about me.

The service kicked off to the tune of a whopping 20 people. The largest crowd it would ever see. Valerie has always supported me and been by my side, but she said I moved out of God's will and refused to attend.

Lesson: Be slow to say, "God said something."

So, every Sunday following the benediction at Kingdom Christian Center's early service, I drove home to pick her and our children up for the main service. It was a complete disaster. The sad thing is, the faithful few who supported me loved me too much to tell me the truth. Finally, I gave in to the reality that God was not going to breathe upon this service because I had the wrong motive. On top of being humiliated, I had to figure out how to end the service after stating God led me to start it in the first place Lesson: Be slow to say, "God said something." Too ashamed to admit how badly I messed up, I announced I'd only started the service as an alternative to the main one for the summer, and it would end by Labor Day. I was so discouraged. Why would God bless other pastors to have additional services and not bless me to do the same?

This fumble taught me not to compare myself to other pastors. Do what God calls YOU to do, and don't be envious of what other pastors are achieving. Was I going to pastor this small church forever? Absolutely not, but I failed to see that. What a gracious God we serve. God will save us from ourselves, which is exactly what He did for me. Had I gotten exactly what I wanted, I would've missed seeing God grow that small fellowship into a ministry that has impacted the world. God's ways are definitely not ours. I had to face it; my frustration caused me to pursue what I thought were

Any church plant lacking a formidable foundation to operate in the will of God is bound for failure.

greener pastures. My motivation was completely wrong and ill-conceived. Any church plant lacking a formidable foundation to operate in the will of God is bound for failure.

Lesson - 2

Don't Expect Everyone To Be Excited About You Planting Churches

To my surprise, while Elizabeth City welcomed us with open arms, surrounding existing churches weren't so excited about our arrival. I'll never fully understand; however, we all know the spirit of competition runs rampant among the Body of Christ. Territory is the chief foundation of spiritual warfare. Contrary to popular belief and erroneous teaching, Satan isn't after stuff. Remember the story of the men possessed by demons in Matthew 8? The demon didn't have a problem coming out of the boy; it asked not to be removed from the territory. The demonic is always after territory, and whenever the Kingdom attempts to take territory, the demonic will respond. Anyone called to plant churches must be prepared for a new level of spiritual warfare. The most discouraging part of the warfare is that the attacks often come from the Body of Christ.

As we got closer to planting the church, several local pastors publicly expressed their concern about us coming to town. In fact, it was said that I hadn't asked permission from the local pastoral conference to plant there. While I am always respectful of community gatekeepers, the call to plant churches is divine and must be sincerely regarded with Kingdom responsibility.

Lesson - 3

Location, Location, Location

Location does matter. The first plant location determines how the ministry or fellowship will flourish. Therefore, it's extremely important to educate yourself on the master plan for the city, plans for future development, and the ethnic demographics of the community in which you are planting.

Once the location is determined, the pastor must consider several things. First, what is your ministry product? Always stop and ask if the area needs your anointing. Of course, the leading of the Holy Spirit is the greatest guide for deciding where to plant, but as the scripture says, faith without works is dead. There should be a marriage of Godly revelation and practical examination in selecting a location. Don't decide to plant based on the potential financial stability of a site or the frustration of senior leadership.

Another point to consider when selecting a site is planting in the right city. Without due diligence, you risk planting smack in the middle of the wrong community. If the primary reason for planting a new church is making more disciples for Christ, then location is vital, especially when the ministry has no brand recognition. Studying the demographics and understanding the culture is vital. Again, our first plant was in a different state. Demographics made the difference and launching there made sense.

Lesson - 4

Know What Fish You Are Trying To Catch

Approximately one year from our projected launch time, I was blessed to join the owner of a local radio station as co-host of his morning show. This gave me the ability to build relationships in the community, understand how it functioned, and comprehend its needs as we contemplated where the new site was going to be.

Successful fishermen select bait based on the type of fish they're attempting to catch. If the product does not attractive to fish, they don't stand a chance of catching them. God has called us to be fishers of men; therefore, if we have not determined whom we are called to catch, the vision won't manifest the way we expect it to. I'm not assigned to everyone, so I don't cast my net where I don't want to harvest. I'll never forget a gentleman stating that he'd never join our church because the church covenant wasn't mounted on the sanctuary wall like other churches. This opened my eyes to people's expectations. It was time to figure out what bait to put out.

It's perfectly all right to determine whom you're not assigned to serve. Ministries make the mistake of trying to be all things to all people, which is impossible to do. Stop it. You must identify your fish and focus on serving that primary demographic. Take our two inaugural sites, for instance. Chesapeake is a middle-class bed-and-breakfast city with a population of 250,000. This type of city is where my anointing flourishes best. While there are many factors considering geographical potential, some of the primary things that should be considered are population, cost of living, ethnic demographics, economic statistics, and population age. We may think urban settings are the only ones with problems and massive community needs, but remember, no matter where they are, every community has issues needing to be addressed. The real question is whether the needs of the community are the areas of ministry you are graced to serve.

Lesson - 5

Immerse Yourself Into The Community

The easiest way to engage a potential community is to identify ways to initiate relationships in a grassroots fashion. Before we fully launched our first site, I started a Thursday night Bible study, giving me the ability to build a ministry with minimal staff and a limited budget. A combination of faith and practicality should determine goals and objectives for the new site location. We decided that we wouldn't pursue planting there until we had 50 people attending Bible study consistently.

Even when I evangelize today, I meet people where they are because it's proven to work.

To get familiar with the community and our demographic blueprint, we were at the National Guard Armory, which was across the street from a basketball court. One night, I asked my wife to take over the class so I could go to the basketball court and play ball with the kids. Sports is an easy way to bond and get to know each other. Playing with kids allowed me to meet those who may never otherwise have stepped foot in the church. The same youth I took time to bond with later led the charge in tilling the ground for our plant to thrive. Even when I evangelize today, I meet people where they are because it's proven to work.

Identifying organizations and people who influence the community is an effective way to become visible and market your new site. When researching potential locations, consider local colleges and universities and intentionally build relationships with their leadership. Civic organizations and local politicians are also vital conduits in helping new plants develop and succeed. You can never be overeducated on the city you want to be a part of. The more you discover, the more God will release and sharpen the vision.

Again, demographics heavily come into play to prevent you from forming unrealistic goals for your new ministry. Areas with low means of income can't be expected to match the income of those in the medium to high range. At over 100 years old, our main campus is located in a middle-class neighborhood, hailing some of the highest incomes in our state. On the opposite end of the spectrum, the population and income of our first plant site are significantly lower. Same purpose, different means.

Lesson - 6

Facing Economic Challenges

When planting in areas with economic challenges, it's important not to measure the site's success based on financial dynamics singularly. Instead, your mission is to meet the community's spiritual needs, with an understanding that your site could require ongoing financial support from the main church. The Mount works diligently to ensure each of our sites is self-sustaining and financially independent by their second year of existence; however, there are sites we've had to sustain as well. In this case, the plant's financial sustainability becomes part of the planting church's overall budget.

There must be a balance between sustaining a site and holding leadership accountable for its growth. When they work hard to develop the site and mature the saints according to the vision, I have no problem with the main campus supporting its other sites. But to indefinitely support a church where the leader appears to be less than committed and hard-working financially is not good stewardship.

Lesson - 7

Consider the Culture

Culture is driven by context. Every community's culture predates your church's arrival. Without considering the culture you're moving into, you're making a grave mistake. Lack of proper planning causes the church to become a microcosm of the very community it's been called to serve. For example, planning our Elizabeth City launch showed me that the hospital and a historically black college were the largest employers in town. Armed with this vital information, I immediately began supporting the university and made myself visible at important events in the community. The assimilation process for the new plant becomes much smoother when you peel back the layers and find ways to impact the community and show the value you bring to the table. Trying to burst on the scene without displaying a genuine desire to serve and assist in uplifting the community will prove detrimental to your ministry. Show them what you got and what you can do for them.

Chapter 5

Creating Pastures - Our Current Model of Church Planting

I have learned there are several ways for church sites to be planted and established: total autonomy, hybrid autonomy, or no autonomy. We've defined **total autonomy** as a planted site and becomes a stand-alone, with no day-to-day, legal or financial relationship with the planting church. A **hybrid autonomy** is when the church is planted but has a limited legal or financial relationship. It has some ability to develop the vision and shape the ministry based upon location and needs; however, there are areas of church operations that are pre-determined and managed by the headquarters or main church. **No autonomy** is when the church is planted, but site leadership has no authority to develop or shape the ministry. The main church determines site management.

While all three methods work, we've found that the contextual differences between sites, locations, and leadership styles make it hard to operate under a one-style-fits-all umbrella. The Mount, therefore, adopted a hybrid autonomy. As a result, there are some areas the site pastor does not have the authority to change or adjust, and some in which they do.

Our planting method is patterned after Chick-fil-A's business model. Chick-fil-A's owner/operators cannot decide, for example, to open on Sundays or adjust the menu without approval from headquarters. However, they have the authority to manage, hire and fire staff, and maintain their budgets. This model works for the chain, and since implementing it into our systems, it has worked for The Mount.

When establishing multiple locations, the site pastor's boundaries must be clearly defined and communicated to protect the church brand, provide consistency between the sites, and reinforce the main church's core values. This is especially true when all the fellowship sites are deemed *one church*. Everyone easily embraces the *one church* mantra until the guidelines aren't clearly and definitively communicated and reinforced in writing and practice. No matter what Chick-fil-A franchise you visit, customers expect the chicken sandwich, nuggets, and salads to taste the same. Likewise, we want parishioners to have the same expectations of The Mount, regardless of which campus they visit. We understand that each site won't be physically identical to the next, and the praise and worship may differ. Still, we strive hard to ensure the basic core values mirror each other, so when people exit the door, they can truly say, "We have been to The Mount."

Let's examine the similarities between planting a new church versus transplanting a plant in your home. Most people will take a piece of the old plant, nourish it, and then place it in a new pot. Yet, it never ceases to amaze me how every time a plant is transplanted, it blooms in the new pot and grows to higher heights simply by being nurtured from a piece of an existing plant. It's the same when you plant a church; it will bloom where planted with the proper support. There are, however, several topics that require addressing for both the main church and the planted church to thrive.

Even though the new plant has a safe, fresh, comfortable space to thrive in, it's imperative to keep the original plant healthy and strong enough to handle losing a part of itself before repotting. The same concept applies to church plants. I've witnessed ministries that began planting before they were strong enough to handle the hits that come along with it. Before the new church is planted, the home church is responsible for analyzing the potential impact the launch could cause with tithes, offerings, and attendance as partners transition to the new site, especially when the site is within close proximity to the existing church. In addition, financial responsibility, staffing needs, and leadership development must be adequately planned as the repotting (*planting*) begins.

The inaugural group of volunteers who assist with the new church plant should view themselves as mentors to staff assigned to the new campus. The start-up team then becomes the bridge between both churches, importing the cultural DNA from the old to the new. These mentors aren't bosses lording over the new church partners. Instead, the start-up team is in place to serve and assist in any way needed for the new ministry.

> **Remember that it's important not to assign titles or delegate positions initially at the new site.**

Launching the new site calls for an all-hands-on-deck approach to setting up the sanctuary, running projectors and cameras, and the like. No matter how big or small the task, every volunteer is necessary for helping to make it as seamless as possible of a transition. Remember that it's important not to assign titles or delegate positions initially at the new site. Titles convey responsibility and authority. The new church needs time to define its staff's roles and appoint responsibilities and authority to the appropriate areas and people. Granting titles too soon can cause confusion and conflict and grant authority to someone who's not ready for it. Instead, focus on developing core values and the giftings of those tapped as leaders for the sites.

Remember, everyone isn't able to handle the first chair. Many of us are incredibly gifted at managing a site yet not setting the pace and vision required to be a leader. It's up to leadership to fit staff into the roles where they are most effective. As the new ministry matures, faithfulness will be displayed, gifts will be revealed, and competencies will be made clear. Until they've been appropriately vetted, build confidence by allowing people to serve, and letting the Holy Spirit reveal who should be formally placed in leadership functions.

In solidifying our model, it became apparent that once again, as in the past, The Mount's governing documents did not align with the new church structure. For example, our church constitution failed to mention handling multiple sites and the Office of the Bishop. If you recall me saying, we are still congregationally governed. Our Council of Elders and the Budget and Finance committee cover pastoral accountability; however, we host an annual meeting for our partners to be informed of the fellowship's statistics and vote on church initiatives. We conduct this annual meeting because our governance structure is different from most large churches where a board governs. In our model, the ultimate authority rests in the hands of the congregation. The congregation grants authority to different groups and individuals to lead the church and reserves the right to remove and adjust levels of authority.

Therefore, our *legal* constitution and by-laws had to be revised and ratified by the congregation. Originally, our governing documents were written to address the traditional model of a joint board. Our documents needed to reflect our new model and speak to pastoral authority, recognize the Office of the Bishop and incorporate church planting. I dare say that many churches have not updated their legal documents, even as they have embraced changes in organizational and operational structure and leadership. Now, our revised documents legally and clearly define the lines of authority for bishops and church plants. The Presiding Prelate is the chief overseer of all sites in our structure. Site leaders respond to his directives as employees of the fellowship serving at the bishop's discretion. In addition, leaders are appointed or removed by the bishop. Every church should legally outline and protect its regulations in writing. The official documents must align with the ministry's structure, articulating detailed expectations and roles.

Please understand - that church planting is still relatively new to us. We are still working to define our standards while allowing each site pastor to shape their ministry. In light of this, we've created a full-time staff position called *Minister of Compliance* to ensure each site adheres to The Mount brand. This position is responsible for visiting the various sites to ensure compliance with established core values and standards. For example, some of our sites have a stronger warfare emphasis, while others emphasize commitment to the community or evangelism. While each of these areas is important to the growth of the fellowship as a whole, we deem every site's flavor important. Like multiple children in your home, all have different personalities, and we've allowed for the variations by installing rules that everyone must respect yet remain open to each site's individual needs and priorities.

Realize that everyone will not fit into every ministry's structure; therefore, deciding and appointing leadership at each site is very important. Finding the right pastor to fit the site is a prerequisite for success. For example, urban settings drastically differ from rural ones. Never underestimate the need to match the gifting with the context.

A Spirit of Order and Unity

A church cannot be planted without unity of spirit, mind, goals, loyalty, commitment, and objectives. Let me give an analogy. When a couple already has a child, they should plan carefully before having more. I say this because each additional child increases parental responsibility. Parents sometimes struggle to balance the children's various personalities, needs, and desires—a lot like church planting.

Having two sites was much more demanding on The Mount's staff. As we planted more sites, our dynamics had to be restructured. We are still updating our policies and procedures to fit the growth we've experienced. Most of our site leaders tend to have Alpha personalities (stallions); therefore, order of authority and tangible plans to nurture a unified atmosphere must be continually monitored, modified, and enforced. In African American churches, the leader is often placed on a pedestal with their ego fueled by compliments, accolades, and a spirit of competition, creating an atmosphere of division and lack of submission.

In The Mount's *one church/one leader* (Bishop) model, several times a year, the entire fellowship suspends services for leadership training, conferences, New Year's Eve service, and the Bishop's anniversary at the main campus. Ministry partners from each site are encouraged to remain faithful in giving to the particular site if the event is on a Sunday. The unity services include the opportunity for the complete fellowship to serve, worship together, and enhance branding.

A combined choir, a team of greeters, and other auxiliaries work as a single unit because of the fellowship's universal branding and training initiative across each site, which is corporately controlled. I cannot emphasize how crucial this is in building unity and cross-culture. The saints can also accurately see the role of the bishop and the authority the position carries. Since the bishop's office is new, the authority must continually be revisited to maintain unity.

In addition to the unity services, site pastors (and in some cases, their spouses) are taken on a sabbatical at least twice a year for team building, establishing our annual preaching calendar, and outlining our goals and objectives as one body. We believe and have seen that spouses can make or break a pastor and the ministry. So, we believe the church should invest in the spouse's spiritual maturity and professional development by allowing them to come to some of the training sessions and field trips. These sabbaticals allow us to work through any concerns and changes that have or need to be implemented. When planting a church, you're committing to continuous learning. As additional sites are launched, new processes must be outlined, which The Mount did when our number of sites swelled to nine.

Preaching Calendar

There are several models I have observed for delivering the gospel at various church plant locations. In some models, the site pastor may not preach on Sunday. Instead, with the assistance of technology, the senior pastor or bishop delivers the Word from the main location. In other models, the site pastor delivers the message; however, the senior pastor controls the content. Finally, the site pastor is instructed to preach the same sermon the senior pastor delivered from the main location in some cases.

Specific to our model, site pastors are responsible for delivering the Word. We are fortunate to have a solid team of senior pastors who've been formally trained and are equipped to preach with clarity and anointing. However, different voices flowing from the pulpit do not mean we've abandoned our one church mantra. Continuity is important to us, although site pastors have the freedom to preach how they're led. At least twice a year, I assemble all the site leaders to collectively draft a preaching calendar focused on monthly themes to keep us on the same page with our preaching subject matter.

Though most of the calendar's subject matter is planned for the year, we are open to making exceptions as needed. For example, January's focus could be Family, February might be Relationships, and we may discuss Giving and Stewardship in March. But if one of the site pastors needs to veer from the main theme, we will make allowances with approval. The best part is, with all of the leaders working from the same preaching calendar, there's more unity and balanced discipleship across all the sites.

Another reason I bring the site leaders together is for them to share their thoughts in a safe place. Working together to strive for more and challenge ourselves keeps us from becoming developmentally lazy. It demands that we remain open to preaching a holistic gospel message. We believe preaching should be a time of illustration, explanation, and application.

Remember, every preacher and pastor has anointing proficiency in a specific area. Our unified calendar removes the crutch that cripples pastors when they rely on their gifts rather than the Holy Spirit to deliver The Word effectively. Preaching on gifts alone is exhortation without substance. Let's be clear - there is a time for exhortation, but preachers must remember that preaching is the instrument God uses to communicate His message to the church. Therefore, preaching must always be approached with the perspective of being an oracle from God and preaching the entire gospel and not just their favorite scriptures.

Finally, a unified calendar helps us be aware of dates significant to Christians throughout the year and plan for special events.

Transferring Culture

I have always believed that a church takes on the personality of the pastor. If the pastor is a giver, the congregation will be generous. If he is argumentative, the partners will be combative. If the pastor reveres marriage, chances are the parishioners will value the institution, too. We think of the home church (parent) and plants (children) as one family in our model.

The Mount, in some cases, had to contend with the distance between the mother church and our children (church plant). Planting a church minutes away compared to hours presents an entire set of different needs and concerns. The further away the children are from their mother, the more intense the work is to keep them connected. Unfortunately, I've made the mistake of not being as sensitive to the distance and fostering a bond between the campuses as I would have desired.

We've attempted to build stronger connections and transfer a unified culture by introducing what we call The Culture Conference. It is an annual time of training, impartation, instruction, and fellowship for our site leaders. The Culture Conference empowers our leaders and includes a question-and-answer forum so everyone can be on the same page and address in a unified format any concerns. The conference also opens the floor to share ideas from multiple perspectives. Some of our most prominent ideas have been birthed from ministry leaders at the site locations, which shows that just because we've always done things a certain way doesn't mean there isn't a more productive and effective way to get it done. At the conference, there are general sessions where everyone gathers to hear the voice of the bishop; then, we break into small groups to study various disciplines such as music, parking, doorkeepers, greeters, etc. It's an invaluable time that strengthens our core values and fosters a spirit of unity in the greater fellowship.

Additionally, we strive hard to build into our culture a spirit of cooperation and celebration of the successes achieved by every site. The world pushes for winning at all costs and being the "top dog." We combat that worldly view and preserve the unity within the fellowship through the senior site leaders and the bishop monitoring and squelching the spirit of competition. We address competitiveness head-on with a blend of sensitivity and authority. The Kingdom is too valuable to get caught up in any kind of sibling rivalry between locations.

Please note the language used to identify ministries must be consistent across all locations. So for example, our children's ministry is referred to as *The Mountaineers Children's Ministry* at all sites. Implementing this and other language across the fellowship is a gentle reminder to the volunteers that we are, in fact, one church that happens to be in different buildings.

Culture provides a platform that enables the saints to always clearly state who they say they are. Most corporations strive to ensure that the people across the organization can express and articulate their core values. The same goes for the church fellowship, especially when planting multiple locations. Reinforcing culture establishes consistency across each planted site and fortifies our identity. We must know who we are, for if we don't, we will answer to anything.

Know that culture not only strengthens unity, but it also protects your fellowship's brand.

Branding

Your brand defines who you are and what you do. The *brand* is what people say and think about you, while *culture* is what you say and think about yourself. Jesus was sensitive to both. In Matthew 16, Jesus asked the disciples, "Who do the PEOPLE say I am, and who do YOU say I am?"

Branding answers the first question and is important to understand when planting churches and operating as one church in multiple locations. If we are truly one church, then regardless of which church an individual visits, they should leave feeling and believing they visited a Mount Church. Like any other eatery, you expect what you order to taste the same regardless of which store you visit. The facilities may be different in size and amenities; however, each store has a common core value shared from store to store. The same is true for The Mount. Our mantra is "Church is Supposed to Change Lives." We believe The Mount Global

Fellowship of Churches should cover, connect, and care for its partnership. Our branding repeatedly supports our mantra and beliefs.

For example, we are known for our Greeters who will meet you at the door and say, "Welcome to The Mount." Our phone operators answer the phone and say, "How may I bless your day?" With the reputation of being a benevolent church, it is no surprise when spontaneous giving breaks out during the middle of a sermon. People walk up to the platform and begin to place money on it for a special moment or upcoming event or simply because the urging of the Holy Spirit hits everyone to give. You will find this behavior at every planted location because of the consistency of our brand.

Each of our planted locations has its unique style because a different personality leads each site; however, there is a branding culture of worship, good music, and a sound Word at the center of each location. Although our site pastors are given freedom in their Sunday message, the invitation for spiritual decisions and benediction is still the same at each site. In addition, though they leave room for the Holy Spirit to operate, intercessory prayer and altar calls are standardized. As we are only a few years into our church planting, we are still identifying our core values and the standards we want to exemplify at each location. Therefore, each of our site pastors must remain flexible and open to the changes coming from the Office of the Bishop as these standards become the norm.

As mentioned earlier, the Office of the Bishop employs a Compliance Officer responsible for visiting each of the sites to ensure they comply with whatever standards that have been communicated to each site. Oversight and continuity are important to ensure standards do not change from site to site. While site pastors may have great ideas, individual sites cannot haphazardly develop processes that will erode the culture and *one church concept.* New ideas must be shared at the corporate level before becoming a standard. Just as a Chick-fil-A owner cannot unilaterally decide not to sell chicken sandwiches on Wednesdays (while it may be good for that particular store), our site pastors cannot unilaterally do something that has been decided not to fit our branding standards.

When you leave a Mount location, we want you to feel like you had a Mount Experience.

Facility Consistency

Sometimes, it's hard for me to comprehend the marvelous place where God has taken us. I was called to a small brick church that seated approximately 150-200 people; never would I have imagined that we would have multiple buildings in two states and nine locations. Today, we have seven facilities totaling just under 200,000 square feet. Each site is maintained, cleaned, and kept the same by our facilities department, overseen by the Director of Facilities.

Consistently managing the custodial operations of multiple sites can be problematic without a well-thought-out plan and a corporate standard for the condition of the building and cleanliness, which can be as important to the worship experience as the sermon, praise, and worship. Unfortunately, church leaders don't always sacrifice the same amount of time and emphasis on upkeep as we do the platform. Hiring staff to perform intermittent cleaning and minor tasks is the least stressful way to sustain the aesthetics of your campuses. Do not forget to be good stewards and keep up the maintenance. When people drive past your facilities, they should see the excellence of God, not overgrown weeds and cracking paint.

Customers become accustomed and expect to see a certain look, floor layout, and product type sold when they patronize a particular store franchise, despite the city they find the store. The same holds true for the church. There are expectations of commonality when someone enters a Mount site. Several areas of each planted facility must be consistent where feasible when planting churches. Colors, décor, and everything about the spaces should be staged the same when possible. Have you ever noticed how Wal-Mart's floor plan is virtually the same at all stores? They want customers to have the same experience and comfort at each location. Don't you get frustrated when one store is set up differently from the

When people drive past your facilities, they should see the excellence of God, not overgrown weeds and cracking paint.

others, and you have to spend unnecessary time locating items? It may not be possible for you to set up each site with identical configurations because of physical differences in structure but stay as close to the brand as possible. The instrument layout, platform, and podium placement are several ways continuity can be accomplished. Add to that wording, language, banners, lighting, and then you will see the atmosphere become set for your brand.

Minor nuances can affect how people relate to you; nothing can affect culture as much as the images we display throughout our buildings. Pictures are attractive; we attract what we display. This is where appointing a Minister of Compliance helps visually bring *one church* together. The Minister of Compliance orchestrates the images, visits each site, and makes recommendations for changes to uphold the brand.

Our facility continuity strategies go as far as to make sure the marquees outside of the church are the same at all locations. We want our identity to be familiar and recognizable. So when people see The Mount, they know exactly what they're getting.

Interchurch Transfers

Every Sunday, I receive reports from The Mount's sites providing insight into their attendance, the number of saints who answered the call to salvation, rededication, prayer, and partnership. These weekly demographics show me where the campus is and if any adjustments or changes need to be made for improvement. For example, analyzing demographic results showed me we needed to develop a method to account for partners that desired to switch their attendance to a different Mount site.

Thus, we implemented a site transfer process to facilitate the move of partners between locations. A transfer form must be completed if a partner relocates from one site to another. For example, suppose that partner served in a ministry or leadership. In that case, site pastors are personally notified of the transfer, and an exit interview is arranged before the partner is released to change locations. The exit interview is also an opportunity for both pastors to express their concerns about the transition and ensure the leader transferring is in good standing.

Partners under disciplinary action generally do not mention their transgression to their new pastor. No one really wants to say, "Hey – I'm leaving because I got in trouble," right? Without air-tight parameters set in place, chances are that partners will gloss over the fact that they caused conflict and were suspended and jump right into position at the new site without ever saying a word. Oh, it happens. Believe me.

Do you see how this would cause conflict and division between sites? Our policy is that if a partner has not been released to be a leader at any of our sites or serves in any official capacity, that individual will be sitting down when they relocate to the next site until the disciplinary period is over. So, while we can't prevent anyone from worshipping where they want to, we can maintain a sense of order and accountability in our leadership.

Regulating site transfers limits recruiting people for the ministry and competition between sites. Knowingly welcoming musicians, choir members, psalmists, and others onto the platform when they're in a disciplinary period or have caused division and strife at another site can taint the fellowship.

In addition to partners and leaders transferring, I have had to address paid staff who may desire to transfer. The length of service and pay raises caused dilemmas surrounding the compensation of employee transfers. Each of our sites has a budget that they are responsible for managing. Therefore, there are limits and restraints due to budget differences. Compensation across the sites varies, particularly for musicians. A guitar player at one site could earn more or less than a guitar player at one of the other sites, so a lateral transfer may not bring the same compensation. Before hiring, we make it clear to staffers that their salary is based on the budget at the site where they work, which could result in a reduction or increase in the event of a transfer.

Financial Impact of Church Planting

When we plant a new congregation, we request some of the partners from the mother church to assist in planting the new congregation. At times this group of partners is asked to serve at the new church plant for a pre-determined season, maybe one year, for instance. This initial group provides for continuity of brand and core values, and they become a part of the financial support system for the site leader or site pastor. The new site leader needs to remember that they were sent by the grace and authority of the planting pastor. Those who accept the call to be a part of a new church plant are vital to the development and success of the new plant. In the case of a church planting process in which a site pastor is assigned to lead, it must be clearly understood that they are sheep from the planting church's fold. Suppose this is not carefully examined and understood; it can cause financial decisions to be made without completely considering that some financial support was temporary and not permanent.

This initial group of believers from the main church will, in most cases, begin to give their tithes and offerings at the new site. The finances generated from the initial group may create a false reality for the new site, especially if the group does not plan to stay at that church plant permanently. Additionally, a sense of loss may be felt at the main church because of the deficit of the group's offerings, making it more difficult to sustain the budget and cast a contextual funding vision. However, we have found that many who go to the new site usually stay. Mount Ops is responsible for estimating the economic impact of partners transferring to another site, whether temporary or permanent. This should be considered by both the main church and the new site plant.

As a part of our planting process, Mount Ops has learned and advised us that we are not ready to plant an additional site if we are not prepared to invest a minimum of $250,000 per year for two to three years (or more). While we hope, pray, and believe that additional sites will become profitable within that time frame, we have also recognized that developing a new location takes time, effort, and capital. In addition, things such as rental costs for facilities, purchasing acceptable equipment for worship services, supporting staff salaries, utilities, ministry needs, and down payments for new facilities must all be weighed. Therefore, Mount Ops is instrumental in maintaining all records relevant to new sites.

Merging as a Church Planting Strategy

I'd never considered merging congregations until I received a call from a young pastor I'd given my number to many years before. He was in distress about a dilemma he was in. His was a relatively young congregation birthed out of complications; they had found themselves deep in debt. Complicating matters even more was the health issues he was having.

As he poured out his heart, the pastor asked me to do two things: pray with him and visit his church. I agreed to go, but in the back of my mind, I wasn't looking to plant another location and didn't want to get involved in another church's affairs. However, one thing made me realize it was God's will for me to go. His church was in my hometown - Portsmouth, Virginia.

My wife was the only person who knew it was my dream to pastor in my hometown. So, I seriously prayed every day, straddling between yes and no. Finally, one afternoon, I asked Valerie to ride to the facility with me to seek God's will concerning the possible merger. Once we arrived, God immediately confirmed it was His will for us to merge the congregations because they had worked so hard to serve the community. *Okay, God, we hear you. But where do we start?* Planting a church is scary enough, but merging two completely different congregations? It almost seemed impossible. But with God, we all know how that story ends.

Pray for a Witness

Before deciding to merge two different ministries, pray first... you're going to need it. Inevitably, one church is being dissolved and folded into another church. Emotions may be high, and the saints may be sensitive. Make sure to tread lightly in these situations! It may seem unusual to merge; however, as delivering the gospel has become increasingly non-traditional, the Body of Christ has to be much more open to it.

Research suggests that small churches not part of a larger fellowship will cease to exist by 2025. The only way some ministries will survive is to become part of a church network. For this reason, you must pray for God to remove the temptation of flesh and pride to merge based solely on ego. Acquiring a ministry can't be done out of pride and arrogance; it's got to be a situation where both congregations benefit by joining together.

Let's go back to the young pastor and his dilemma. After several days of prayer, God confirmed the merger was, in fact, His will. I'd recently become familiar with a new term - *adoption or blending of church families,* which suited us perfectly. I prefer to call it adoption; we are all the Body of Christ. Coming together as a family can display the common thread of the Body for the world as we unitedly represent Christ by marrying our corporate anointing with one another.

Evaluate The Context

The context in ministry is very important. The anointing that works in one place doesn't always work in another. Mark 8:22 displays context well as it depicts Jesus about to perform a miracle. He immediately recognized that the environment wasn't conducive to effectively serving the blind man's needs, so He led him out of the village before performing the miracle.

Despite years of wanting to pastor in my hometown, the reality was that the city's needs needed to match the collective anointing of our fellowship. As I explored our options, I discovered that many of our Chesapeake partners grew up in Portsmouth. Never force your anointing where it isn't called to go, simply for the purpose of padding numbers. I want to go where God assigns me. Some disciples were sent to the Jews, while others were sent to the Gentiles. Anointing matters. Context matters, too.

Meet With The Merging Congregation

Set up a meeting with the merging congregation to introduce yourself as the leader and start fostering relationships right away. Be transparent concerning who you are and what you're about. The night I met the congregation we planned to merge with was one of the most anointed ministry meetings I've ever been a part of. When I walked into the facility, I was dumbfounded to be greeted by leaders with whom I'd gone to high school. It was awesome to see people I hadn't seen in years. If that wasn't solid confirmation from God, I don't know what else could've proved it was His will.

At the meeting (without breaching confidentiality), I tried being as transparent as possible in communicating pertinent details about The Mount fellowship to put the congregation at ease. Every leader was allowed to introduce themselves and share their leadership roles before Valerie, and I introduced ourselves and gave them a little background about our ministry journey. Never assume people know who you are and the road you've traveled. Tell your story; they need to hear it.

Following our personal history, I explained Mount Lebanon's history before openly sharing where their congregation stood at that time, covering, most importantly, their financial standing. It is important to understand all debts and liabilities you are acquiring and acknowledge areas of vulnerability and lapses in paying bills. Next, we unveiled our action plan, detailing our proposal to make the merger seamless. Once everything was laid out, we ended the evening in prayer, knowing God was definitely up to something special.

Inspect Facilities

One of the most important steps in acquiring a new ministry is due diligence. Before finalizing the adoption, make certain to perform a detailed facility inspection because, as the adopting church, it's now your responsibility. Besides a few minute technology upgrades, the facility we acquired was beautiful, well maintained, and in good condition. We were so thankful we didn't run into the same disrepair other adoptive churches had when taking on a new facility. Know what you're getting into before you take the deep dive.

Keep in mind that the adopting church must be clear on its financial ability to assume the responsibilities of the new church. Will bearing the burden put you in a financial bind? Research existing mortgages, outstanding balances, accounts payable, liens, and active legal suits. Flood zones and flood insurance, the roofing system, and the HVAC system should be examined because they tend to be big-ticket replacement items. A history of utility costs and other variable expenses should also be researched to accurately picture what you're facing. Inspecting the facilities provides insight on the number of staff needed to keep it running properly. When possible, employ a professional inspection service to develop a clearer picture of the facility's true condition.

Consult an attorney if needed about the legal structure of the church. An attorney will advise you of your best options. Still, the customary approach is to never assume the legal entity of the existing church without first knowing the legal liabilities you may be taking on. In most cases, it's advisable to start with a new legal company.

Communicate a Plan

Now that you've gotten things behind the scenes together, it's time to communicate your plan of action to both congregations. Communicating a clear plan kills the spirit of assumption and confusion. Your plan should answer questions like:

> ➤ Who will the leader be?
> ➤ How will existing leaders be accepted?
> ➤ What will the new operations look like?
> ➤ What changes can be anticipated?

Every congregation has positions of equity; how these positions are understood and respected can make the transition much smoother. Although two churches join together, it's akin to death for one church. The congregation

> **The congregation must be given time to process their pain and disappointment as the transition occurs.**

must be given time to process their pain and disappointment as the transition occurs. Don't take it personally if everyone doesn't want to participate in the merger. Respect their feelings and work hard to please God in preserving the witness of the Kingdom at all times.

Respect Existing Leadership

One of the most important components of a church merger is to respect the existing leadership of the church that is being adopted. This is not the time for finger-pointing. Refrain from entertaining conversations that disrespect leaders. The Bible is clear that when we honor biblical leadership, God releases honor and favor upon us. He admonishes in 1 Chronicles 16:22 to touch not His anointed and do his prophet no harm.

Instead, applaud leadership that is honest enough to recognize when their season of pastoring (at least at that location) has ended. It takes a mature individual to release a ministry to someone else. As we adopted our merger church, God instructed me on what to do next.

I met with the founder to pay respect and express my gratitude for his efforts. I also acknowledged that we were standing on the foundation he created and would be benefiting from his efforts and legacy. To my surprise, he informed me that God had spoken to him years before directing him to turn the ministry over to me. As we prayed and bestowed blessings upon each other, God confirmed the steps of good men are ordered by the Lord.

It also meant a lot for us to acknowledge and respect the *church's lay leaders*, accept them as leaders in the merger, and train them under our construct. We were blessed by the lay leaders' wisdom and asked them to continue with us; there was no reason to lose them. Today, I am excited that much of the leadership and laity remain and have become an integral part of the family. We've been able to come together and make an even bigger impact on the community.

As a final part of the adoption plan, we were blessed to take care of any delinquent compensation agreements and ensure that staff was allowed to thrive and continue in the new church structure. Respecting the church's legacy that's adopted and creating a safe space for ministry transition will honor God and allow a new chapter of ministry to be written. Also, trust in new relationships will develop as the two churches come together to serve the assignment of making disciples.

Today the church merger has been very successful. We now call this site, The Mount Portsmouth. My son, James, is the senior site pastor. Once again, this site adheres to the Mount branding; however, because our son is a part of the next generation of leaders, he is unique in his style of ministering the Word on Sundays and his leadership model. This fits our idea of why the planting or merging of new churches is so important. The style of ministry at The Mount Portsmouth may not be successful in some of our other Mount locations. It is important, as discussed previously, that you must understand the context of your site's location for it to be fruitful.

Develop a Financial Plan

Now let's discuss finances. If the church has outstanding debts, communicate with lienholders to tackle how to get the debt cleared and renegotiate if you can. Be sure not to miss any open debts, including tax liabilities and IRS breaches, and put them on a spreadsheet. Seeing it all grouped will help show how to make the ministry financially whole.

Always remember that we represent the image and reputation of Christ. So, when making the ministry whole, don't miss employees who are owed back pay to solidify the relationship between both churches and build respect. It also goes a long way in showing the adopted church how much you care about them.

Chapter 6

Qualifications For Leadership

Successful church planting doesn't happen overnight. While the criteria for selecting leaders can be endless, I believe several specific traits and qualifications are directly required. The Bible is replete with leadership assignments such as Paul and the Gentiles, Matthew, and the Jewish population. Then, of course, there is Jesus. He was so sensitive to the leadership and culture that He could serve lepers, tax collectors, mothers, fathers, and ministers in homes, the temple, and at weddings.

However, David, Moses, and Joshua are further biblical examples proving that every leader isn't birthed; some are created. Perhaps this is because the Bible admonishes us to lay hands on no man suddenly (1 Timothy 5:22-24). Likewise, the Apostle Paul instructs young Timothy in 1 Timothy 5:12, "Never be in a hurry about appointing a church leader" (NLT). I've often been accused of moving too slow to elevate folk, but I will never be accused of moving too fast. I have learned through past mistakes to exercise extreme caution when making decisions that will impact the fellowship. People can fool you in a short period, but patience and time will reveal their true character.

Never promote opportunists who haven't served with a genuine spirit or displayed humility and strong character.

Throughout this journey, I've never sought a site pastor or leader—our leadership graduates into the opportunity. Following Elizabeth City, the next plant manifested in this way. I'd taken a Sunday off to spend some downtime with my family and asked one of our ministers to preach in my absence. Watching that morning's live stream, I witnessed God release a pastoral anointing on that minister. It wasn't just the response of the congregation but the grace covering him as he ministered. Quietly, I began observing without sharing with him or anyone what God had shown me. I casually released small pastoral tasks as a litmus test to see how he would handle them. To my delight, he passed the tests. Never promote opportunists who haven't served with a genuine spirit or displayed humility and strong character. Just because candidates can pump up the crowd and provoke a round of amens doesn't mean they're called to lead. Moving too soon can also move someone into position before they're ready. And the sheep get hurt as a result.

Matching the site leader to a culture that fits their gifting, personality, and life experiences create a bridge for the church and the community to establish healthy relationships and productive ministry. The right individual in the right location is a foundation for success.

Serving as the bishop and breaking off a piece of the main church and repotting into a new church plant is a major decision and requires a great deal of faith and trust in the appointed leader. However, if we are honest, the leadership in the body of Christ has deeply rooted trust problems. Pastors don't trust pastors. Pastors don't trust associate ministers. Pastors don't trust ministers of music. I've learned not to say all. Still, if you've been in ministry as long as I have, you know their trust issues stem from personal hurts and past bad experiences or from stories told to them by other pastors. So again, appointing the right person is crucial to the success of the ministry.

Years ago, I heard Bishop T.D. Jakes says he doesn't promote anyone who has not gone through the fire with

Always examine the fruit and the fire.

him. Therefore, every leadership candidate needs relationship collateral, which I call the *"fruit and fire."* Always examine the fruit and the fire.

Fruit

Long before I was licensed to preach, Pastor O.L Cromwell, Sr., told me I was a bootlegged preacher or preaching without a license. Since then, I've always looked to provide opportunities for other bootlegged preachers. Let me explain: Those who serve without being formally recognized are the ones to watch. Their pure service shows that their call is already being developed. There are so many people who lead and disciple without the title, a supreme display of faithfulness. I've noticed preachers who've made the best pastors are those who were unofficially pastoring. Here's a good example - at The Mount, our youth pastors were serving, leading, and developing young people before I acknowledged them as youth ministers and before they formally got the title. It is very dangerous to promote anyone who hasn't displayed the fruit before the elevation. Matthew 17:16-17 makes it clear, "You can identify them by their fruit, that is, by the way, they act. Can you pick grapes from thornbushes or figs from thistles? A good tree produces good fruit, and a bad tree produces bad fruit" (NLT).

FIRE

Relationships that can't handle challenges and disagreements (fire) aren't strong enough to partner together, much less plant a church with each other. No matter how close they believe they are, they will undoubtedly butt heads on how to lead their ministries. This is normal; however, the ability to have disagreements and emerge from the fire unscathed needs to be tested. The strongest relationships will survive when we understand these dynamics and learn how to navigate storms. Because most pastors shy away from conflict, we tend to ignore bad fruit.

> **Valerie has taught me not to believe who people say they are but the person they show me. Period.**

Valerie has taught me not to believe who people say they are but the person they show me. Period.

While the word loyalty isn't used in the Bible, faithful is. Faithfulness is the sum of competence, character, and submission. Therefore, your candidates must display consistent faithfulness, first to the Kingdom and then to leadership. According to Matthew 25:21, the Master was full of praise. "Well done, my good and faithful servant. You have been faithful in handling this small amount, so now I will give you many more responsibilities. Let's celebrate together" (NLT).

As leaders, we tend to emphasize the servant's faithfulness yet overlook the servant's good. I've seen many people who were faithful but not good or people who were good but not faithful.

> **I look for people who are both good and faithful.**

If someone is faithful to you as a leader but not good for the culture, they may not be the person to lead. I look for people who are both good and faithful. Too many leaders are faithful to leadership, but their character is weak. We can't promote people with a limited view of faithfulness; it must be measured by character and competence, balanced with submitting to the organization's vision and the bishop. When considering leadership qualifications, I begin by having them serve in roles where their commitment can be observed and measured.

Never promote without proof.

Gifts alone aren't the reason for promoting people. You don't want to overlook them, but it's just as dangerous to promote someone who can't be corrected or disciplined. Conflicts are inevitable; if a team member can't be corrected, they don't need to lead. Never promote without proof - seek the opinions of multiple sources before promoting anyone as a leader. As the Bible declares, in a multitude of counselors, there is safety.

Your new leader MUST embody the *spirit of attraction* - which means others are attracted to their gifts and engaging personality. Preaching and teaching alone will not grow a church. The leader must be charismatic. Every great preacher is not a pastor. Every teacher is not a pastor. Sheep are attracted to pastoral gifts. Your pastoral candidates should draw people to the Kingdom.

Leadership Titles

Titles define authority and set order in the house. They're not badges worn as a source of pride but a burden reflecting responsibility and accountability. Currently, there are four titles The Mount Global Fellowship of Churches (MGFC) bestows on our leadership team: site location leader, site facilitator, site pastor, and senior site pastor. The bishop has the authority to appoint all of these positions, which do not operate in any specific order of progression or promotion. Instead, their purpose is to differentiate lines and levels of authority. Each position answers to the bishop and is deemed part of the bishop's staff. The congregation does not take part in appointing or governing the site's leadership or any of its employees.

Site Location Leaders

A site location leader is a lay leader who serves under the supervision of a senior site pastor. They are the point person who handles the daily tasks instead of the senior site pastor. While the location leader isn't a licensed and ordained minister, there's a strong possibility they'll be asked to preach at the senior site pastor's discretion. Lest I run the risk of offending the religious and fanatical, being licensed and ordained is not a requirement for sharing the gospel but a source of guarding the faith and building accountability in the Kingdom. In addition, the site location leader can be used to perform counseling and other ministry responsibilities with the senior pastor's approval. We began to use this title because we found that tremendous ministry gifts were being stifled because they don't have a proper title, certificate, or license when needed for services. We believe that if you can meet the ministry's objectives and needs, it doesn't matter if you don't have a title or license. Our experience has been that site location leaders ultimately become licensed and ordained.

Site Facilitator

The site facilitator is also unlicensed and not ordained. Unlike the location leader, the site facilitator has authority over a particular site, is accountable for setting the site's vision, and is directly managed by the bishop. They can hire and fire staff, manage site operations, and share the gospel in addition to developing, training, and overseeing ministry volunteers. They can take disciplinary action where they deem fit, counsel, and handle sacerdotal responsibilities.

I will admit that this position was birthed out of a battle with my religious baggage. When we merged with the existing congregation in Portsmouth, this unexpected blessing swooped down so fast that we didn't get a chance to groom a site leader. My full plate didn't leave much room for me to assume the leader's role myself.

Yet, this was too big of an opportunity to let slip through my fingers, so I consulted with my good friends, Dr. Sam Chand and Dr. Leo Whitaker, who had the same solution to my dilemma: appoint my biological son as the pastor. I was intrigued but not fully prepared to give my son such massive responsibilities, even though he'd been in church his entire life. Maybe I didn't want people saying it was nepotism or personal baggage, but I wasn't ready for him to take this on. He hadn't even expressed an interest in pastoring, nor was he licensed. However, he had earned a Master of Divinity Degree from Samuel DeWitt Proctor

School of Theology at Virginia Union University - one of the leading seminaries in our nation.

I wrestled with the decision like Jacob fighting for his blessing. Still, eventually, the Holy Spirit confirmed it was the will of God for us to acquire the facility and that my son needed to lead the charge. I heard what the Holy Spirit said, but I was still apprehensive. My son and I share the same conviction to serve the Body of Christ and demonstrate integrity and character, but our similarities end there. Our styles of proclaiming the gospel and ministering to the people are completely different. In the end, he was appointed pastor of The Mount - Portsmouth, and my spirit was put at ease.

> **His success has shown me how our preconceived perception of leadership can cause us to overlook gifted and qualified leaders.**

It's been amazing to watch my son develop and witness how the congregation responds to his leadership. Pastor James or Simba, from the movie The Lion King, as seasoned partners affectionately call him, is quick to tell you he's not a preacher or teacher – he's a *conversationalist*. Pastor James believes the Mount Portsmouth is Church Redefined. His success has shown me how our preconceived perception of leadership can cause us to overlook gifted and qualified leaders.

Site Pastor

The Site Pastor is licensed but not ordained. The first year of a new plant is considered a mission of the planting church rather than a stand-alone site. After that, the pastor is appointed and given a year to prove that the church will take root and display fruit. Finally, the trial year will show if the pastor can lead and sustain a congregation.

The site pastor is typically appointed before senior leadership fully invests in the site financially. It's much easier to shut a site down before investing capital, acquiring a permanent facility, and hiring a full staff. These methods have helped The Mount expand and soar far beyond what we originally envisioned. We are confident in our vision for church planting; however, there will always be answers that won't come until the new site has been opened and operating. Do not be afraid of redirection if leadership fails to prove themselves or the site does not grow as planned.

Senior Site Pastor

In our model, senior site pastors are licensed, ordained, and the highest in command. This pastor assumes the responsibility of running the church and reports to the bishop over the fellowship. They are a mature, proven leader who has displayed the ability to grow the site, whose pastoral gifts are visible, and whose commitment to the vision has been tested.

The Role of the Presiding Prelate or Bishop

The primary purpose of the Office of the Bishop or the Office of the Presiding Prelate is to provide vision and governance for the fellowship. In the same way, Jethro advised Moses in Exodus 18:13-26. He was tasked to find capable and honest men (and women) who could assist him with his heavy burden. I, too, have found some capable men and women to assist me with the heavy burden of the ever-expanding fellowship. The Office of the Bishop establishes a governance structure with staff to maintain a united fellowship and operate in excellence. This office establishes and enforces all policies and procedures, thereby assuring consistency of the Mount brand and compliance to the fellowship's standards.

The Office of the Bishop serves as the hub for all policy and guidance for the fellowship. It creates and disseminates all standards and procedures to ensure uniformity of operations and ensures financial stability. These standards and procedures are reviewed and revised as needed.

All staff serves at the pleasure of the bishop, and the bishop has the authority to hire, fire, and appoint leadership at the various sites. The bishop is the leader and serves as the Chief Apostle of the fellowship.

Compensation of New Site Leader and Staffing

The Mount Operations LLC is responsible for preparing all paperwork related to employment within the fellowship. Every site pastor must sign a written employment agreement that includes standards of character and morality as we believe the lack of either should not be tolerated. The agreement is clear on how moral failures will be dealt with, including disciplinary action. The relationship between the site pastor and the bishop must be strong to manage any issue that may arise accordingly.

One area where integrity and morality are most crucial is finances. The site pastor is responsible for the site's budget and financial accountability, which must be handled with credibility. Likewise, tithes and offerings are sacred and must be conducted that way.

So, let's talk about employees. All staff - including senior site pastors, are employees of the fellowship. Site employees should have state and federal taxes withheld from their checks and should be mailed a W-2 at the end of each year. Upon being extended a job offer, employees receive a written letter from the executive pastor outlining their job description, benefits (if any), and annual compensation, which is paid bi-weekly. They should also receive a packet containing the following:

➤ Employee handbook (benefits, policies, and procedures)
➤ Federal and state tax forms (W-9 and VA)

> Direct deposit authorization

> Job descriptions

> Offer letter

> For senior site pastors, the packet also includes: A non-compete agreement, dictating the terms of separation.

This is a great place to reiterate putting everything in writing. Habakkuk 2:2 says to write the vision and make it plain. When expectations are clearly documented and discussed in advance, no one can claim amnesia regarding the terms of the agreement because things happen, relationships change, and situations arise. If employment terms are properly planned and agreed upon in the beginning, the split can be amicable without unnecessary stress. Unfortunately, the body of Christ has often been guilty of murky policies; ambiguity breeds a lack of order and accountability.

Despite our best practices and planning, we can still get overwhelmed as we navigate through our assignment, which ultimately reflects the love of Christ on Earth. In the meantime, employees want to know about their money. So, you have to plan if and when your new site pastor will be compensated as a full-time staffer and what additional staff needs hiring.

Mismanaging your new plant in its first year will cause it to be a financial burden to the mother church. The Bible is clear that the servant is worthy of his hire (Luke 10:7). However, in most cases, hiring a salaried pastor full-time in a new plant isn't good stewardship. If the pastor is motivated by money and getting paid, they may not be inclined to nurture and grow it.

Don't get me wrong; most pastors work full-time with or without a full-time compensation package. They're on call 24-7, and partners contact them at all hours, disregarding the pastor's life outside the four walls of the church. They are expected to respond at all costs, visit partners during times of distress, and push everything aside to make someone else's emergency their own. However, suppose the pastor works a secular job, balancing all of these events piles on the stress, and the lack of sleep can create health challenges. Whether they work an outside job or not, it's all overwhelming.

Tempering the best financial interest of both the church and the pastor is a delicate situation if the pastor must work a job outside the church. Striving for this situation to be a temporary norm, The Mount Operations LLC has constructed a full-time compensation package, including (but not limited to):

> Base salary
> Housing allowance
> Benefits

  ‣ Health insurance
  ‣ Dental insurance
  ‣ Life insurance
  ‣ Disability insurance

- Car allowance
- 403 B retirement plan
- Accrued annual and sick leave
- Federal holidays off with pay
- The week between Christmas and New Year's off with pay
- Continuing professional development

It's our preference to employ site pastors full-time; however, many church plants have limited resources that need consideration. You don't want to burden a struggling ministry with the pastor's salary and benefits. We encourage new site pastors to start by being involved in outreach to attract partners to their locations. Then as their resources grow, the site is able to compensate the pastor accordingly.

A pastor friend simplifies the compensation process with this observation in his church plants: His pastors can only eat the fish they catch. Remember, a man who doesn't work doesn't eat. Motivate the new pastor to take an active part in growing the ministry and then allow him to enjoy the fruits of his labor.

I've made a personal commitment not to present an offer to an employee that I wouldn't accept myself. This mentality has served as a guide for how we compensate The Mount's staff. Unfortunately, churches have become known for underpaying or asking people to volunteer rather than being fair and equitable about paying

> **I've made a personal commitment not to present an offer to an employee that I wouldn't accept myself.**

their worth, especially if the church can afford to do so. Therefore, we recommend that staff salaries be part of the budget set at the top of the year.

Chapter 7

Mount Operations LLC - Centralizing Operations

The Mount's operating structure includes centralized Human Resources and Financial Management operations handled by a separate entity we established called, The Mount Operations LLC. This entity is 100% owned by the Mount Fellowship, and the sole manager is The Presiding Prelate over the fellowship. However, as staff increased and our number of sites multiplied, we couldn't ignore the need for an additional formalized structure and an organized system of policies and procedures. Therefore, the Mount Operations, LLC, commonly known as Mount Ops, operates as headquarters for all sites for everything dealing with human resources and the finances of the fellowship.

Mount Ops updates the employee handbook with the standards of conduct and procedures and outlines employee benefits. The church is notoriously known for failing to handle employees and finances with excellence. However, most churches eventually find out that the church is limited in its growth opportunities without excellent stewardship and the management of resources.

Unfortunately, employee concerns aren't a problem until there's a problem. Safeguarding and keeping good records can save the fellowship unnecessary hardship when dealing with disgruntled employees. In addition, putting it in writing removes ambiguity and prevents selective amnesia when confronting conflict.

Every ministry should be Christ-centered, but that doesn't absolve us of liability. Every decision we make must be done responsibly and in order. Being reliable requires meticulously documenting every practice of the church. Standards, budgets, employee relations, and every process the ministry implements must be uniformly stated for everyone to see, know and understand without debate. This protects the church both morally and legally. Whatever is in writing is more difficult to dispute.

"In God we trust; all others check out thoroughly," I once heard Bishop I.V. Hilliard say. "The people of God will steal God's money." Unfortunately, this is a sad but true reality. Your standards set order in the house and shape the culture. Make it plain and maintain the fellowship's credibility as a whole.

Let's face it; the church doesn't necessarily have a stellar record regarding finances. So as part of our checks and balances, we streamline everything through Mount Ops.

Receipt of Contributions

Currently, over 80% of our contributions are given online. We use apps that directly interface with our financial software, so that contribution information is captured at the point of giving and posted directly into the donor's records and posted and deposited into our bank accounts. In addition, any funds given at each site during offering or otherwise are handled by appointed counters. They count, bag, and deposit at the site level. Finally, a standard reporting form is completed and forwarded to Mount Ops for processing and reconciling with the bank accounts.

Disbursement of Funds

Mount Ops does all disbursements of funds. All vendor invoices and vouchers for internal check requests are mailed to Mount Ops. The Fellowship identifies those individuals who are authorized check signers; all checks require two signatures. The bishop nor the site pastors have check signing authority. Despite their inability to sign a check, each leader does, however, have the authority to approve vouchers for disbursements and payments. It's a basic system to keep checks from being written or disbursements made without the approval or knowledge of at least two to three individuals. Even with approval, adequate documentation must be attached to support it.

All we have is our reputation and our credibility; both are important to us across the entire fellowship. We pride ourselves on operating in integrity and having our partners' confidence that the church's funds are being safeguarded to the greatest extent possible. Of course, no system is 100% theft-proof, but we inspire our staff to be vigilant in their duties. As long as they do their job and follow protocol, we should be able to detect fraud to at least minimize financial exploitation easily.

The Mount Operations, LLC does the following (including but not limited to) for every site:

> Processes payroll bi-weekly
> Prepares monthly financial statements, including a Balance Sheet, Income Statement, and written financial narrative, which includes changes in cash balances
> Processes vendor invoices and pays the bills
> Opens and closes bank accounts, reconciles them monthly as each site has checking, saving, and investments accounts (if applicable)
> Reconciles internal fund transfers and ensures payments are made internally
> Receives and deposits donations, posts them to partner accounts for year-end donation letters, and reports them weekly to site pastors
> Prepares year-end tax forms, including W-2s, 1099s, and donation letters

- Coordinates the annual audit and acts as a liaison to the external CPA firm
- Reviews contracts and formal documents for services rendered. Seeks legal counsel where deemed appropriate, acting as a liaison when needed
- Manages cash flow
- Negotiates mortgage loans with banks and manages banking relationships
- Coordinates obtaining Trustee signatures on formal documents
- Sets up and manages online giving
- Establishes retirement accounts and manages insurance policies (property, health, dental, disability, cyber, and life). Maintains employee files
- Establishes individual site budgets and consolidates all budgets when deemed appropriate
- Sends site-specific financial statements to each Site leader and meets with them at least once a month to respond to questions regarding their financial reports
- Manage corporate credit cards and reconcile receipts monthly
- Prepares official Offer Letters for Employment to potential new hires
- Conducts credit and background checks on all employees
- Creating the organizational chart for employee reporting
- Determines the need for the creation of additional LLCs, including securing IRS identification numbers

Have I mentioned that my wife, Valerie, serves as Executive Pastor of the Mount Global Fellowship of Churches and CEO of The Mount Operations, LLC? She is the other half of 'we' that I've mentioned throughout this book. All of our success is God's doing, which goes without question. However, The Mount nor I would be as successful as we are if it hadn't been for Valerie's love, passion, pure heart, expertise, and anointing. Many churches use the title, Executive Pastor to mean many different things. We use that title to identify the authority of the individual responsible for all the executive arms of the ministry. Some people have a problem or concern with naming or using family members within the church in leadership roles. Many will use the term nepotism to describe this action. However, nepotism is "the practice of showing favoritism toward a family member without regard to merit." The keywords here are 'without regard to merit.' Valerie wasn't given her positions because she's my wife or without regard to her merit, abilities, and skillset; Valerie is qualified. She is a true executive pastor in every sense of the title. Once again, it is amazing how outsiders can recognize and use abilities and skills that we will not take advantage of within the church. Although she's been in full-time ministry since 2000 and isn't currently practicing as a CPA, Valerie's financial expertise put us in a position to plant churches and do things right. She earned her CPA license in 1980 in Virginia. She earned her Doctorate in Management from The Weatherhead School of Management, Case Western Reserve University in Cleveland, Ohio. She has worked in Public Accounting with the International Accounting Firm of Arthur Andersen and several corporations. Elder was actually overqualified when God told her to close her CPA practice to work beside me for free. She was the founder of her very successful CPA practice for fifteen years with several employees before working for the ministry. She was the first Black CPA in private practice in Chesapeake when she opened in 1987. God definitely called her. I don't know too many people (anyone, actually) who would've done the same.

When questioned about our Fellowship's policies and procedures, checks and balances, organizational structure, and financial acumen, I simply point to my wife. She has truly been my helpmeet and is more than qualified to assist me in leadership. Valerie provides wisdom and counsel to me whenever needed. I also say, "if I can't trust my wife, who can I trust? She surely has a vested interest in the ministry doing well because if it goes down, we both go down."

PART II

Kingdom Legacy for the Family

Chapter 8

Family Legacy

When it comes to the family, the 23rd Psalm has always interested me because the Psalmist declares, "He maketh me to lie down in green pastures." This implies it is not automatically the desire of sheep to embrace and lie in green pastures. Just as the shepherd with his sheep, so are parents with their children. Before lying down, however, children must first be led; there should be a road map of some kind. Where the family goes, green pastures should be clearly defined with goals and objectives. Without them, how will you know you have arrived at the appointed destination?

Faith Legacy

Over the three decades of ministry, I have observed Christian families, particularly pastoral families, often lack balance between their faith and functioning as ordinary people. Some children of believers (especially pastors' children) act out and rebel because church has been forced down their throats 24 hours a day, and they feel they have missed out on a normal life. There is still a great debate between what is defined as church behavior and expected behavior. This does not simply apply to children but to adults as well. However, I want to focus on the children right now. I believe the Bible when it says, "we should not copy the behavior and customs of the world" (Romans 12:2). However, this scripture is not referring to kids being kids and enjoying childhood, such as playing games, spending time with friends, enjoying sports, and other wholesome activities. Too many times, I see adult Christians who did everything under the sun as children suddenly find Jesus and then stifle their children in fear they will repeat the *everything under the sun* behavior. Instead, these same adult Christian parents should be teaching their children which behaviors are unacceptable and why. Valerie always tells me to never forget when we were young and how we thought when we were their age. We try and bring that knowledge into our conversations with our children and listen to them. You want your children to want to please and respect you. Your children don't enjoy a set of rules and regulations they are required to follow no more than we as adults want a set of rules and regulations to follow. We all simply want to understand what is acceptable behavior to God and why the Bible is our source for all these answers; not man-made rules and regulations.

When I became a Pastor, my children were still very young. We worked hard to make sure they did not feel church was a priority over them. We were also diligent in helping them understand that life involved more than church work. There is a difference between church work and Christ. We always taught that Christ was to be first in their lives, not church work. Too many pastors and believers have not learned how to balance church work and daily living for the next generation. I am proud that I was my son's first basketball coach and that I was my daughter's room Dad during middle school. Please never forget that Jesus spent time doing other things than preaching and teaching in the synagogue. He spent time at weddings, visiting friends, and sleeping on boats. Every day cannot be consumed with ministry. Too many believers have raised children who know how to pray, lay hands and speak in tongues, and do the *holy dance* in church but cannot hold a pleasant conversation about life. Every statement they make, regardless of the context and environment, includes statements like, "praise the Lord, to blessed to be stressed, and hallelujah." A simple, "how are you today?" elicits the response, "blessed and highly favored." What happened to "I am doing fine, thank you." Don't get me wrong. I do not believe there is anything wrong with such sayings; however, there is a time and a place for everything (Ecclesiastes 3:1). A football game or in the grocery store may not necessarily be one of those places. I remember when my son and I attended an event with another pastor and his son. As we returned home, I asked him how he enjoyed spending time with the pastor's son. My son shared that while he seemed to be a nice guy, he felt he could not have a regular conversation because everything had a biblical answer no matter what they talked about. It could be football, basketball, or school; everything was a biblical response. He wanted to say to the other son, "relax and be a normal kid." This might seem strange to some of you reading this chapter, but my children hang around people other than church kids. Maybe that is the disconnect. If all you hang around are church folks, maybe this language is okay for you. But please remember, while your children are attending school, they are not simply hanging around church kids. If we are called to minister to the *unsaved*, we will surely need to learn how to have a regular conversation with non-church folks. My children have brought more kids into the kingdom than most adults I know. That is because they are typical kids. They don't go around quoting scripture in every sentence, including biblical phrasing. It is because they show unchurched people that you can love Christ, live for Christ, and still enjoy life. The Bible tells us to seek the Kingdom first, but it never tells us to seek it *only*.

I am proud that our two children are actively engaged in ministry as adults and did not run away, revolt, act out in any way, or dismiss their spiritual upbringing and teachings. Don't get me wrong. They were by no means angels. They got in trouble. They were disciplined. But we allowed them to be children; each of them arrived at their ministry assignment by enduring the process and journey of their call without always quoting scripture. While parents are called to give guidance, we should never overstep the boundaries of the will of God. Please allow your kids to be kids as they grow up and have confidence that God will order their steps. One of the greatest ways to accomplish this is by consistently *modeling* a balance between our faith and adult lifestyles. Modeling respect and reverence for the Kingdom while enjoying life is critical. What are you modeling before your children?

As parents, it becomes important to observe where our children's gifts are being displayed and create opportunities to develop those gifts. Our son has always been an independent thinker and antagonist when embracing norms. He was never afraid to ask, "why?" This is why, today, the congregation he leads redefines how church looks and operates. While Jesus Christ is still the center of the church's ministry, their methodology is very different from what I was raised embracing.

Platform Legacy

The greatest thing a parent can give to the next generation of kingdom legacy is a platform. Every profession creates a family legacy. Morticians, politicians, doctors, dentists, and founders of businesses, are some examples of legacy planning for their families by encouraging and motivating their children to follow them in the 'family business.' It is a biblical principle that we, as kingdom leaders, should be doing the same for our families (Numbers 3:5). God has allowed me and my wife to grow a ministry platform with great influence. God has a requirement and mandate that the ministry does not end with us. We should encourage and motivate (not force) our children to want to follow in our footsteps and serve in the kingdom. We should be creating a pasture for which they can do this. We are Levites, and our bloodline calls for service in the kingdom.

As believers, we should be mindful of developing strategies for the next generation to embrace their faith in salvation and practicality. Every generation should not have to start from scratch. Leaving an inheritance for the next generation is more than just money and land; there should also be a spiritual inheritance. This applies to all parents, not just pastoral parents.

Have you thought about the call on your family? What is the assignment that God has placed upon your bloodline? Discuss with your children why your family was placed on the earth. Serving in the kingdom goes beyond the four walls of the church. Help your children understand that we need kingdom-minded teachers, preachers, doctors, accountants, lawyers, bankers, etc. As I started to survey my congregation, I was amazed to see the children of soldiers become great soldiers, the children of bankers become next-generation bankers, and sons and daughters of educators who have become academic administrators. God has always desired the family to be the conduit for the legacy of faith. Noah's family was saved. Rahab's family was saved. The very terms matriarch and patriarch have legacy implications.

We should not limit training our children about faith to simply dying and going to heaven. Instead, we should be attempting to train up the next generation of Kingdom leadership, ministers, and servants. We never pushed our children to be in full-time ministry, but we did make it clear that our family is called to impact the community and world for Christ. Spend time talking to your children about their kingdom assignment. Help them understand that whatever they are called to is a kingdom call from God. Begin to assist them in seeing that they have disciples and followers who follow their lead. Help them embrace that they are expected to be leaders, not just followers.

I suggest that we raise the next generation with a kingdom consciousness that informs whatever they feel led to pursue. They are *kingdom* teachers, doctors, nurses, etc. I believe that every individual has a pulpit. It might not be inside of a church. Their pulpit can be in a classroom, an office, or any other place in our society. Our children's first jobs were at the church, not for pay, but to model service. It would be sad for a family to never discover its Kingdom assignment and recognize its Kingdom value to the world. Model faith, introduce faith, allow your children to see you serve the Kingdom, and submit to the call of the Kingdom on your life. You don't have to shove the Kingdom down your children's throats. All we as parents need to do is model before our children what kingdom service looks like every day. Remember, more is caught than will ever be taught.

While most pastors spend time developing their spiritual children, they seem to forget to develop their biological children. Enlist others in the Kingdom to give you advice and support in nurturing the spiritual journey of your children. When my son was in high school, I leaned on a good friend, Pastor Leo Whitaker, to assist me in directing a decision my son was making. The old proverb is true; sometimes, someone else's ice is colder than yours. Although I may have said the same thing Pastor Leo said to him, it was only when someone else said it did it penetrate through to my son. During my son's teenage years, it was clear that he was wrestling with decision-making and the challenges of being a pastor's son and living in a bubble. Pastor Whitaker met with him at his high school and simply gave affirmation to his future. However, confirming his future in ministry was never a roadblock for him in enjoying his teenage years. The bottom line is this. You, as a parent, must have established guidelines and rules for your household. We told our children they had to behave and do or not do certain things because that was the standard of the house, not because they were the *pastor's kids.* Don't put that pressure on your kids. As I reflect on their journey, I am thankful for all those who stood beside my wife and me to assist in their spiritual formation.

Creating a platform for the next generation's faith also means defending your children when needed. Because I realized my children were being called into the ministry, it became clear that Satan would attempt to frustrate them into not fulfilling their spiritual legacy. I clearly remember being approached by someone who was disappointed that their kid informed them that my children were seen in the club. Let me say it again. *Their* children were in the same club as my children. I very diplomatically defended them by stating that fact as well. Please never allow your children to become victims of a spiritual double standard. Truth be told, it was probably the fact that my children were in the VIP section of the club (I knew the owner) that really was the concern. It is possible to allow our children to live normal lives, enjoy their childhood, and become the Kingdom vessels that God desires. It is all about the standard you set within your household. Help them to know the boundaries.

Perhaps you are saying I don't have a platform to provide for my children. Nothing could be further from the truth. Simply stated, your platform is whatever influence, relationships, and partnerships that God has allowed you to develop. I started to understand that one of the simplest ways to introduce my children to my platform was visibility. Take your children with you to platform moments. Be very intentional in leading them to green pastures. Expose the next generation to the individuals and circles that have produced the platform you stand upon.

One of the most valuable platform assets is relationships. Don't allow relationships to die with you; leave these relationships to your children. If you study most legacy organizations, relationships are valued very clearly. Fraternities and sororities express this better than any legacy criteria for the next generation. I have introduced my son to my ministry platform, and he is now developing his as a result. His young son, too, has already been introduced to his ministry platform. I pray that God allows me to see who my grandchildren are called to be. I plan to leave them well equipped to complete whatever that Kingdom assignment may be.

Sacrifices

——— ..

I have observed that we often do not allow the next generation to become aware of the required sacrifices of legacy. They embrace the legacy and enjoy its benefits but are unaware that much is required (Luke 12:48). Children need to understand that providing a platform and ensuring legacy is not an entitlement. They must earn the platform. While I agree that each generation should not have to start over, please know that starting at the bottom for every generation is essential in their growth. There is a difference between starting over and starting at the bottom. That which we do not work for, we will most likely not appreciate. It is unhealthy to start at the top because you have nothing to be motivated to achieve. Although David was a King, he started by tending sheep and taking cheese to the battlefield. You must kill the bear and the lion before you are given the platform to kill Goliath.

To make sure your children are ready for the platform, give them floor assignments. Our children started by putting labels on cassette tapes (dating myself), being teen camp counselors for fifty dollars a week, playing the drums for twenty dollars a week, delivering meals to the homeless, and serving in shelters. This prepared them for the platform and gave an opportunity for gifts to be exposed and sharpened. As parents, we must ensure that we do not sell the next generation short or expect them to be like us. Can I also say that the reverse can be true? I have found that because I have had to work so hard to prepare the platform that I have, I selfishly want the next generation to pay their dues before enjoying the benefits of kingdom platforms. This should not be the case either. We must remember that if every generation has to start over, we will limit the amount of kingdom territory than can be taken by future generations.

Spiritual formation is different from person to person and generation to generation. Allowing others to become aware of your spiritual journey and belief system will enable the next generation to recognize their call and expedite their progress. The Bible says it this way, "we all must work to make our calling sure" (2 Peter 1:10). Your children will each have their journey and paths to take. It may not resemble your journey. Your job is to ensure you have instilled the basic principles of life in them so that they have a toolbox of wisdom when challenges are presented. Just as we are all created with individuality, our journeys are unique. Stop allowing your journey to prevent you from assisting the next generation in arriving at the place of kingdom maturity. Remember, not one of us got there overnight. Fulfilling the kingdom assignment is a marathon and not a sprint.

My wife and I have a non-profit named K. W. Brown Ministries, Inc. T/A, Keys to the Kingdom Ministries, and our children serve on the board. They don't serve on the board only because they are our children; they serve on the board because this allows them to learn how ministry operates and to see first-hand how non-profits impact our community for the Kingdom of God. Because they sit at the table and assist in making ministry decisions in our non-profit, each of our children now has non-profits themselves. They each are impacting our greater community by serving the needs of women, young ladies, and young men. Not only do they sit at the decision-making table with my wife and me, but their presence brings fresh ideas and prevents us from becoming stuck in traditional viewpoints of ministry that are no longer effective.

Whenever I hold my grandchildren, I cannot help but wonder who they will become in the Kingdom of God. I want them to understand the assignment on our bloodline, and I desire to live long enough to see how God plans to use them. We are priests in the household of faith. We serve people by serving the Kingdom. It is not simply giving them a name but a kingdom consciousness that will live long after I am gone from the earth. Joseph did it for Jesus. Abraham did it for Isaac. Jesse did it for David. You and I are called to do it as well. Whatever you do, do it as unto the Lord (Colossians 3:23-24). We don't just teach our children to have a career but to have kingdom impact, be world changers, and continue to provide a family legacy platform. I challenge you to think about the platform God has allowed you to build. Inspire the next generation to embrace their call, grow the family legacy and leave a mark that can never be erased.

Finance Legacy

Unfortunately, I have discovered that we don't teach all the critical things our children need to know to be successful in life. We leave spiritual teaching like praying, serving, integrity and character up to the church; Sunday School when we were coming up. We leave life lessons to the public-school teacher or lessons learned on the playgrounds. How many of you have said or heard others say, "I wish someone had taught me that when I was younger before I made all these bad decisions." Who teaches our children about finances? I have story after story of breakdowns in generational legacy when it comes to finances.

Much of the financial dysfunction in the Kingdom (world) is because, for generations, it was a *learn-as-you-go* process of education or the myth that the kingdom believer was supposed to be poor like Jesus. The topic of Jesus' finances is discussed in greater detail in Valerie's book, *The MisEducation of the Christian*. It is clear that many economic instructions have never been taught and much of the kingdom confuses operating by faith with not practicing sound financial principles. While I agree that we are called to live by faith, I am also reminded that faith without works is dead. I am asked many times when one should begin to teach and leave a financial legacy for the next generation, and the answer is the day your child is born.

Then make them stick to it.

It begins in early childhood. Something as simple as providing an allowance in their early years needs to be understood as a vehicle for training our financial mentality. Think about this for a moment; an allowance is money that parents usually give to children weekly or bi-weekly. Remember, as parents, we are called to train up a child (Proverbs 22:6). An allowance can be used to teach the budgeting process. Impart to them; their allowance is to be used to pay for small things they may want, save for larger purchases, and give to God. Then make them stick to it. If they decide to spend all of their allowances needlessly, do not allow them to come back to you to get more money before the next allowance payout. Don't teach them how to use payday loans or pay advances or ask for their paychecks before payday. Remember, everything is a lesson. Share with them that they must wait until the allowance is due again and learn to live without. Always ensure they pay God first and never allow them to spend before doing this. You should also ensure they save some. Most banks will allow a kid's account. Take them to the bank to open their account, and each time they make a deposit, show them how their cash balances are building up. Help them identify a goal they would like to save for. So much satisfaction will be achieved when they can buy for themselves, whatever their goal may have been. You can even start with a piggy bank at home. Then when the piggy bank gets full, take them to the bank to open an account or make additional deposits. You will be amazed at how exciting this is for children. It is never about the amount of money you have, but what you do with what you have. If you begin to train your child on these three basic premises, they will carry this life lesson over into their adult life. As our children grew older and wanted more expensive items, we told them they had to save an agreed-upon amount of money that went towards the purchase. This helped them value what they worked for and realize the principle of delayed gratification. Too many children and adults never learned this principal lesson. Today, so many are in credit card debt because they purchase items they cannot afford with instant credit. Once you learn it is okay to wait and save, it carries on into many aspects of life. Anything good is worth waiting for is a lesson best learned early in life.

One of the greatest ways to leave a financial legacy for the next generation is to model sound financial principles before our children. As a part of their ongoing stewardship, our offspring should be required to give tithes from their allowance/wages. Every Sunday, we made sure that ours presented an offering in church. They would accompany my wife to the altar to give or put their money in the offering plates. They not only did what we told them, but they saw their parents model the giving of our increase to the church.

When our children were very young, they were required to give to the church and others in ways that taught them the power of giving. One of the most memorable moments was at Christmas when our children were required to give to people in the community

> **It's simple; it cannot be do what I say; it must be do as I do.**

anonymously. They purchased a new hat for a senior in our congregation and left it on her porch on Christmas Eve. She never knew who gave her the hat but would wear it to church most Sundays. She even requested that she be buried in the hat at her death. To this day, my children still remember her wearing it weekly. I am always amazed by people wearing designer clothes in front of their children but do not give a homeless person any money when passing them on the street. Your example displays generosity in front of your children. Our children were introduced to a spirit of giving by watching us give. It's simple; it cannot be do what I say; it must be do as I do.

As our children began to mature, we also felt that it was important to teach them other financial lessons. They were taught the art of negotiating by being present when we would purchase vehicles. They were also invited to join us at the attorney's office when we were closing on home loans or when creating our family trust funds. These moments are invaluable in establishing financial literacy. Again, instructing our young ones early about economics will benefit them as adults in their financial decision-making. Too many adults still don't understand what depreciating and appreciating assets are and how our economic system works. But it's not too late to learn.

The biblical story of the prodigal son taught me a valuable lesson that I think is worth sharing. The son did not want to wait until the death of the father to receive his inheritance and so requested his inheritance early. The father gave the son his inheritance, and the son was not wise and was soon without any resources. I believe the purpose of an inheritance is to build generational wealth. If building generational wealth is the purpose, it does not have to be limited to death benefits. Parents can help by assisting with down payments on homes and establishing good credit parameters for them. However, it must be noted that we should not make the mistake of the prodigal father and provide financial inheritance before the son has proven to be ready to steward the finances sufficiently (Proverbs 20:21 NLT). I am proud that our children are buying homes and building their generational wealth through real estate, savings accounts, retirement plans, and the stock market. They are not waiting for us to die to achieve wealth. Our death and inheritance will be a bonus to their already established family financial legacy. I have always believed that becoming a parent meant you were your child's greatest teacher. I am a professor of life. But too many times, we are teaching bad habits financially that simply perpetuate generational financial bondage.

What happens when, like the prodigal son's father, you have been committed to establishing financial wealth for the next generation, but they have not matured enough to receive the inheritance. Perhaps those situations demand a different approach, such as establishing a family trust. Placing real estate and cash reserves in a family trust can be a method of making the next generation prove themselves before receiving their inheritance. My wife and I have established parameters for our children and designated a trustee to assist them in stewarding our family financial legacy with set ages at which they could receive certain funds beyond paying for education.

As shared earlier, good financial decision-making must be taught and modeled for the next generation. Student loans have become a crippling trap to create financial bondage for generations. Many parents are afraid to take a stand about college because, at times, they live their dreams through their children's lives. Upon finishing undergrad, our daughter had dreams of attending a certain university to complete her MBA. However, another very good university committed to providing her with a full scholarship, room and board, and a stipend. Although this school was not her preferred choice, it was the best choice. Today she has an earned doctorate with no student loans and is thankful that her parents did not allow her to attend her first choice. She attended the second-choice school, received a quality education, and made lifelong friends with no debt. Although she was considered an adult (over 18), she was still a child in understanding finances. She had no life experience understanding the magnitude of what debt of that caliber would mean to her future. We continued to be the parents and said, "No." Unfortunately, she has friends who are still paying off student loans they wish they had not taken out. If she had shackled herself to student loan debt, she would not be as far advanced in her financial strength as she is, such as the ability to buy a home on her financial strength. While I am aware that, at times, student loans are a necessity, they should be thought about with credible counsel and guidance. For example, a schoolteacher's salary does not change because of an Ivy League school. Leaving undergrad with 100 thousand dollars worth of debt to obtain a 50 thousand dollar a year job is not sound financial decision-making. Many people start in a hole financially because of student loan debt and cannot dig their way out.

Another simple way to build generational wealth is through life insurance. I am often in awe of how many people die without life insurance. Before buying life insurance, research and education must be done so that there is a clear understanding of the difference between term and whole life insurance products. Properly assigning life insurance benefits is important as well. Leaving a major life insurance benefit to children or family members that cannot be trusted to steward that blessing properly is not a sound choice to make. Once again, this might be something that needs to be explored by engaging an estate planner or estate attorney.

Early on in our ministry, we asked young couples to allow the church to insure them (the church is the beneficiary) with the expectation that this would be a way to endow the church for future generations. We did this only with those who had proven to be committed to tithing. Today, it has positioned our church with legacy funds for the next generation as our congregation

> **A vision that can be accomplished by one generation is not a godly vision.**

ages. The cost was nominal and affordable because it was done when the couples were relatively young and healthy. A vision that can be accomplished by one generation is not a godly vision. God makes it clear that He is the God of Abraham, Isaac, and Jacob. God thinks multi-generationally, and we must as well.

Recently my wife informed me that she had to file tax returns for our grandchildren. I was amazed and did not understand why as they are not old enough to work. She had to file returns because when they were born, we established (UGMAs) investment accounts and began to manage simple stock transactions on their behalf and in their names. We took the lessons we learned from her father to another level. My Father-in-law would provide United States savings bonds for his grandchildren rather than a lot of toys on their birthdays and Christmas. So, we decided we would do the same for ours. Before you are motivated to go out and begin establishing and purchasing stock, I need to share some wise counsel. First, you are not ready to invest in stock if you have not established a sound savings process and successfully saved at least six months of expenses. Secondly, you never invest what you cannot afford to lose. For example, you don't invest mortgage payments. Finally, remember investing is not magic or a get-rich-quick scheme. Investing must be done with a strategy and with, sound counsel, and with long-term planning. There is much to be considered because many investment firms can have hidden fees and other costs of which you must be aware.

We have worked to develop a financial philosophy that shapes how we handle and make financial decisions. Because of the influence of my wife's financial background, we live by the following financial convictions:

> ➤ **Give God His first.** Without running the risk of preaching, tithing teaches us to reverence God and use discipline in managing our financial resources. Ten percent belongs to God.

> ➤ **Ten percent is saved for the future.** Here is where you build up your emergency saving account (3–6 months of your monthly expenses should be in an easily accessible savings account.) But after reaching this goal, you should continue to save for funds to start investing in the stock market, increase your retirement giving, planned vacations, a second home, and extra resources to minimize your use of credit cards.

> ➤ **Ten percent is used to be a blessing to others.** How many times has the pastor asked you to give something extra to a special project, and you wished you had it? How often have family and friends needed help (your parents), and you just did not have the funds to help, but you wanted to? The Bible says, "give and it shall be given unto

you..." (Luke 6:38). We all like that as long as we are on the giving end. But YOU must give first. Show God you are a generous giver, and you will see your blessings flowing back to you far greater than you ever gave.

> **That leaves 70 percent to live on.** You might not be able to live by those percentages today, but this becomes a great goal to work towards. This principle will empower you to become more financially sound in the future. For decades, we have operated our home and the ministry by this principle. Simply stated, the greatest key to leaving a financial legacy for your church or family is discipline.

This approach to finances has provided a sound financial foundation from which we have been able to accomplish much for the kingdom and our family.

Every generation should be positioned to go further than the previous generation. Unfortunately, too many people are driving or living in the next generation's inheritance and articulate support for this type of thinking with faith implications. While I firmly believe that God desires for us to live an abundant life, I do not believe that God is pleased with us living that life at the expense of leaving a legacy and inheritance for future generations.

To spend your life working and not have something to show for the years of labor is not fulfilling the mandate of God to be fruitful and multiply. Multiplying is more than having children. I believe it is the intent of the Almighty that we multiply in all areas of our life: physical, spiritual, and financial. Before making decisions, pray and seek sound advice. The lessons I have learned should not have to be learned by my children. I don't want to get to heaven and receive a partial well done. I desire to hear the Lord say well done in leading the ministry. I want to hear Him say, "Well done in leaving a legacy for the church, and well done for leaving a legacy for my family."

Mind (Thinking) Legacy

There is something that is much more valuable than leaving money. That is the education and principles that shape the way we think. People perish because of a lack of knowledge. Leaving a legacy means doing so with wisdom, vision, and not just money. With wisdom and insight, they can generate money (Proverbs 8:11). Romans 12:2 reminds us to be transformed by the renewing of our minds. Our minds, especially those of our children, must be shaped to think appropriately. We have found that *common sense* is not so common. Too many children (adults as well, but a topic for another day) lack the ability to think critically. We must realize their minds are being shaped daily by the things they see, watch on TV, listen to music or otherwise, and the environment in which they live. Therefore, we must be diligent in talking with them every day about everything. My children tease my wife about how she can take even the smallest occurrence and make it a life lesson. We aren't talking about a formal sit-down and teaching a lesson. We are talking about when you are watching tv together, and something happens; use the illustration to make a life point. When you are driving in the car, and the conversation lends itself to a particular life lesson, use that opportunity to share your thoughts and ask them their thoughts on a particular topic. While they might not readily agree with you (and you should not be trying to make them agree with you), they are listening. These conversations are seeds that will grow later in life. We are amazed how our children will remind us of conversations that impacted their thinking years later.

My wife even repeated to our daughter and son certain responses they should be prepared to give if they encountered certain situations in life. Then, every time they left the house, she would remind them of the responses. Finally, our kids got so frustrated and would say, "we know, we know." Yet, they will tell you today they are grateful for those reminders because the encounters came up.

My wife has even shared some of what she calls her worst bad decisions in her life with her children. She explains that she shares this stuff 1) to remind them that she had not forgotten when she was their age, 2) not for them to throw it back in her face later (oh, no, my kids know better than that), and 3) to share the consequences of those decisions and hopefully enlighten them not to make the same bad decisions. She says to them, "at least make a new bad decision. Learn from our mistakes so that you can go further in life." We, as adults, cannot be so ashamed of our past that we are unwilling to share our life's journey for the benefit of our kids. They really will appreciate you sitting down and sharing with them. They will begin to see you as a parent that can be respected and truly loves them enough to open up and be honest with them. Your children know you are not perfect; stop acting like you are and always have been.

When creating a green pasture for your children, always remember the goal is to provide a foundation that gives them a leg up financially if possible; but more importantly, a mindset grounded in Christian principles that will create for them a way of thinking that provides opportunities to take more territory for the Kingdom of God.

Conclusion

The Pursuit of Success

People pursue the proverbial carrot of success in today's environment with three distinct difficulties. First, success is never an overnight reality. Too often, when you do not know or recognize people's journey, it would appear that they have obtained overnight success. I have one request for everyone who will embrace the process of success found in this book. When you tell your story, tell the whole story. Don't give people the highlights of your process that read well and sound good. Share the ups and downs, the hills and the valleys, the passes and the failures, the moments of joy and sadness. The disappointments and lessons learned are all valuable points of instruction and inspiration. For the first ten years of ministry, I was simply trying to maintain and sustain what God had placed in my hands. Many lessons had to be learned, and many relationships had to be cultivated on the road to success.

I always share that no one joined our church in one year of ministry. There are not too many pastors who will share that kind of information. This level of transparency gives others the strength and fortitude to pursue and persevere, be patient, and wait. At the same time, the University of Life teaches and completes the journey.

Secondly, success is not organic; it does not naturally occur. There is a process to success. I believe that there are some universal steps to the process of success. While I don't suggest that these steps are comprehensive, I believe they are a basic starting point and foundation for pursuing and defining success. If you study people in any station of life that have obtained a measure of success, I believe the process has been consistent. Common threads can be discovered from the CEO to the minister that have fed their business, career, and family success. Finally, I have personally witnessed people who were successful in business but failures in life, or successful in their career but failing at family. What a tragedy to leave a great legacy in your career but have unresolved pain and wounds in your family. God desires for us to have an abundant life, which involves all areas of our existence. Our goal should be to prosper in every area of life. Success is a journey, a process, and each person's journey and process are different. The journey is a race, but not a race against another person. It is a race against yourself. Once we discover that we are not trying to out succeed anyone, it produces the mentality of personal responsibility and the conviction that we must hold ourselves personally responsible for success. I fully believe that no one can control or prohibit my success. While I am not naive about the existence of systems and structures that are averse to my success, I fully believe that the self-determination to succeed will always trump the systemic realities of our society. In short, if you want it badly enough, develop a plan, and preserve with patience, and you will become successful.

Thirdly, the definition of success is vague. Success is not measured or determined by material possessions, bank accounts, or popularity. Success is a personal choice that must be measured by a personal definition. It becomes the responsibility of every person to define what their success looks like. The small church pastor is no less successful than the large church pastor. The middle-class parent is no more successful than the one working multiple jobs to make a quality of life for their family a reality. When you begin to define success personally, it relieves the pressure of meeting other peoples' expectations and falling victim to the spirit of competition that is rampant in our society. I believe a basic starting point is to recognize six steps that are foundational to a path of personal success. As the final inspiration for creating pastures and leaving a legacy on the earth, I pray these steps release untold masses into the reality of personal success that God has ordained for each of us. Don't allow society or anyone to define or determine your success. In fact, if you have read this book, you have already proven that you are successful.

The six stages I would like to share are:

- ➤ Lean
- ➤ Listen
- ➤ Learn
- ➤ Limp
- ➤ Limit
- ➤ Lead

Lean

When God gave me these steps to success, I believe He started with lean because it defines a personal position of posture. When we lean against something, it changes our position. In contrast, I am always fascinated when I hear people use the statement; I pulled myself up by my bootstraps. I challenge you to sit down on the floor and attempt to get up by pulling on the straps or laces to your shoes. You will find it is physiologically impossible. I clearly understand that many have put in the hard work and endure processes of perseverance to obtain success in life, but I suggest that obtaining any measure of success is never achieved without support from someone.

One of the greatest lessons I have learned about success is to be careful who you lean on. Let me clarify by using the term lean. By leaning, I mean find those people or individuals that God has determined to use as revelation role models. I promise you that you are not the first person to dream and feel inadequate or overwhelmed by God's dreams in your heart. Find and ask God to reveal who you can lean on. I don't mean to look for a person who can financially or physically support you. Many years ago, I visited Crenshaw Christian Center Church in California. I remember my brother-in-law and myself sitting in their television production area in amazement that a church had accomplished so much through the leadership of one man, Apostle Fred Price. My ministry journey has been filled with moments like that. These people became those that I leaned on as examples, patterns, and models. I have discovered that people can become models and mentors, and I never have to be physically in their presence. I like to say it this way when people ask me how I became so successful; I tell them, "I have people." I have a long list of people that I have leaned on over my years of life. Begin to look for your people as well. Look for people you can lean on in all areas of your life, family, career, parenting, etc. You need people. I use the term lean because I believe you have to incline yourself to observe individuals who have obtained a reasonable level of accomplishments to embrace and understand the requirements to achieve success fully. Once this principle is identified, you will be amazed to discover God has already positioned people that you can lean on. In fact, I submit that they have been there all the time. Once again, this does not mean that you hang out with them, vacation with them, or even establish a formal relationship. They are examples to be studied, models to be followed, and patterns to be duplicated. When I worked for the government, I leaned on Betty Bates. She taught me about management, plans of action and milestones, and goal setting and measurement. In ministry, I have leaned on Pastor Joe B. Fleming where I learned about the value of staff and ministry benevolence. With Bishop I. V. Hilliard, I gleaned the importance of family and integrity. The late Bishop Eddie Long was instrumental as I discovered the theology of the Kingdom of God. As I play the movie of my life, I can point to people that God placed in my life that were there to provide individuals for me to lean on. I'd like to pause and ask, who are you leaning on?

Can I let you in on a major secret? I have learned that arrogance is the greatest enemy to success.

Arrogance will fool you into believing that you are already successful and that you don't need to lean on anyone. Arrogance is the vehicle used to convince the driver he or she has already arrived at their destination. But do we ever fully achieve success, or are we constantly pursuing and redefining it based on the season of life we are in? Success at 20 looks different than success at 60. Success as a single looks different than success as a husband or wife. I have come to understand that success is an elusive achievement. The moment you think you are successful, I think you begin the process of evaluation and fresh pursuit based upon new goals and direction. God calls us from grace to grace, from faith to faith. As I reach the end of the runway in my career of pastoral ministry, I now recognize that I must establish benchmarks for what success looks like in the next chapter of my life. I don't want to only be successful as a Pastor. I want to be successful as a grandparent, bishop and church planter, and community agent of change. One of the most exciting components of success to me is the process of redefining and refocusing life dreams and goals and establishing processes for new seasons and new opportunities.

I don't want to only be successful as a Pastor.

Listen

My grandmother used to say that God gave us two ears and one mouth because we are supposed to listen twice as much as we talk. Some of the most meaningful lessons I have ever learned became possible because I sat in rooms and listened. Unfortunately, listening is, in fact, a lost art in today's society. Learning to listen is a product of self-discipline and humility. Unfortunately, many are not effective listeners because they have bought into a false reality about their pool of knowledge. Simply stated, they think they know everything, and no one can teach them anything.

Listening is a great identifier. You can learn so much about a person by simply listening to their conversations. Many years ago, I heard a statement sitting in the back of a sanctuary in Atlanta that still impacts my life today. The conference speaker said, "more is

> **Too often, we overlook these moments and belittle their potential impact on our destiny because we take them for granted.**

caught than taught." Actively being silent and listening can open a time of clarity and instruction from the Holy Spirit; this time will have a lasting effect in all areas of life. One of the gifts that God has perpetually provided for me is the entrance into rooms of significant people. What a privilege to find yourself in rooms where you are not the most intelligent or gifted. I often tell people that you have outgrown your circle if you are the most intelligent and biggest fish. It is healthy to always position yourself in circles and environments that push and stretch you to pursue the next level of excellence. I actually walk into these moments like I'm attending college. Just as you listen in a university setting, rooms are classrooms; there is much to grasp and understand. Life presents us with various classrooms and many professors. Whenever ministers or staff accompany me into these moments, I always ask upon our exit, "What did you learn?" Too often, we overlook these moments and belittle their potential impact on our destiny because we take them for granted.

All listening is not passive. Many times, God sends people on your journey with the sole purpose of speaking truth and direction. Before I go any further, let me clarify that everyone is not someone that qualifies to listen to. The Bible declares that in a multitude of counselors, there is safety. Therefore, it is advantageous for everyone to have a circle of truth around them - people who genuinely provide constructive criticism. The operative word is constructive. Honest criticism should always have at the root of

> **The most effective counselors are those who have nothing to gain from the relationship.**

its purpose to build and not destroy. The level of progress in life is directly correlated to having true counselors giving us advice and direction. The most effective counselors are those who have nothing to gain from the relationship. Therefore, they are not intimidated to speak the truth. When I am confident that my counsel has nothing to gain by desiring to see me become successful, it creates a relationship culture of confidence. Successful people are not intimidated by the success of others. These people love to share insight with those they see the potential for success presently in.

Train yourself to listen intentionally. Keep records of lessons learned and who they were learned from. Record the rooms and gatherings that have given you life, career, and spiritual revelations that have impacted your destiny. Never forget that God uses people from all walks of life to be adjunct professors to us. If you approach and ask any successful individual how they got where they are, without a doubt, they will point to someone who shared insight, gave them direction, or simply spoke a word of encouragement and listened.

Learn

Before I move into learning as an integral component of success, I need to clear up a misconception. Many think listening and learning are the same. However, I believe they are very different in application. How do I know when I have been taught something? The evidence of learning is application. When the student can apply what has been taught, learning has obviously taken place. Valerie always says she never had to be taught a lesson by life twice; she learned the first time. Some of us, however, learned by the school of hard knocks. As I look back over my 60 years of life, I have some great life professors both in and outside the kingdom. Every day that the Lord blesses us to be alive should be embraced as another day in the University of Life. At the end of every day, two questions should be asked and answered. The first question is. What did I do to make the world better? And secondly. What did I learn today about myself, my gifts, anointing, and call? Some of my greatest lessons have also been some of the simplest lessons. I am also convinced that many lessons go unlearned because they are minimized in value or not recorded for future reference. Keeping a lesson journal can assist with this for sure. The Bible says that the Word of God is like a seed that must be planted in good ground and protected to prevent the birds from coming and stealing it. I believe lessons are the same. Many lessons that we learn are, in fact, for future reference and therefore must be stored for future reference marks. Because lessons are learned daily, monitoring what we listen to and who we fellowship with daily becomes important. Many lessons can be learned by simply observing the activity surrounding us as we accomplish daily assignments. Lessons on giving, for example, can take place in the check-out line at a grocery store. Much of learning is also a result of personality. By this, people who do not believe they need to learn more or continuously limit their learning capacity. Individuals who are experts in all areas usually have fooled themselves into a place of perpetual ignorance. Humility is the foundation of learning. Learning is a statement of intellectual submission. To learn requires a student and elevating someone to the position of teacher. I am amazed that most of their time together, the men who followed Jesus referred to him as Rabbi or teacher. There is so much that can be learned vicariously simply by adjusting perspective and postures about learning. Becoming a unilateral student and being open to lessons from all types of people will provide a platform for accelerated growth and development. For example, when I see a homeless person, I learn to be grateful and persevere.

Too many people limit their ability to learn because of an arrogant posture of existence. A key component of becoming a continual learner is to do a personal examination and acknowledge an area of weakness. When I am honest with myself and understand the areas where I am weak, it informs the lessons that need to be learned. Remember, the key to learning, I believe, is changing behavior or applying lessons. For example, if I need to learn lessons on giving, I focus my study on givers and their behavior.

If I need leadership growth, I study leaders. While this sounds so simple, it demands that individuals be honest, responsible, and hold themselves personally accountable for their growth.

Developing a learning mentality can become the platform for new levels of education. When I enter a room, I expect to learn lessons. I set my attention on acquiring what I need. I see a room full of teachers. Every moment presents itself as a teachable moment if we adjust our thinking and expectations. Whiles others are socializing, I am learning. I am working on life degrees in psychology, group dynamics, decision-making, leadership, team building, etc. More times than I can say, I have found people from the streets who were much better trained as leaders than those who have attended high-dollar seminars and been trained by professionals. Informal learning can prove to be pure. Unexpected lessons are many times the most valuable. Keeping my ears and mind open creates a mental culture of learning.

Furthermore, authentic learning always begins with the acknowledgment of weakness or limitation. Lesson storage is important as well. Lesson storage occurs when I force myself to apply the lessons learned to my behavior. Lessons on giving, for example, must be practiced. When I don't practice the lessons I have learned, they are forgotten and lost. The ongoing practice of the lessons that we learn informs our behavior and decisions in the future. Lessons are not simply about knowledge; lessons and learning are about the future decision-making capability of an individual. The old folks used to say it like this; when you know better, you do better.

Eternal learners are also always changing. When people say that you have changed, we should be excited because that means we are learning. Romans 12:2 makes this clear; we are transformed by the renewing of our minds. Renewal is a continual process. For example, my son is teaching me about parenting by how he is raising his three children. Observing him, I have absorbed so much about parenting, relationships, and my calling. Anyone and everyone can teach us if we are open to instruction.

When I was in school, I hated homework. After spending all day in school, I never understood why we had to go home and do more learning. Later I began to understand that it was designed for positive reinforcement. Taking the lessons that had been taught that day and applying the lessons that night communicated the student's progress. The first thing in the morning, we would hear the teacher say, "pass your homework to the person on your left or right," so that it could be collected. The grading of the homework was not the teacher trying to bruise our ego and self-esteem; it was the teacher allowing the student to be honest about the educational progress. Grades never really surprise the teacher; they inform the student. The grades allowed the student to recognize that the lesson had been learned or needed more study time. We all learn differently and at a different pace, but I have recognized that many lessons in life are sequential. Just as you cannot learn algebra without learning simple math, many simple life lessons must be learned before we can address more mature lessons. As believers, it becomes very clear that God uses lessons as opportunities to display preparation for more responsibility. All lessons have a behavioral objective. My progress in my kingdom assignment and anointing is directly connected to learning prescribed lessons on my journey. Once again, God teaches us line upon line and precept upon precept. Kingdom maturity has little to do with how long one has been a disciple but how productive they have been in learning. While we often acknowledge the word disciple through the lens of followship, it must also be understood from being a student. The disciples were students of Christ. I believe my success in life should not be measured by years or by material possessions but by the manifestation of changed behavior resulting from my learning experiences.

Limp

I often wonder about Jacob. The Bible says that Jacob wrestled with the angel of God until his hip was dislocated, which caused him to walk with a limp.

Why would God cause Jacob to wrestle and leave him with a limp? Maybe the limp was not punishment but publicity. Perhaps the limp was a memory for Jacob but ministry for everyone else. The experiences that cause the limp are vital for the limper and equally important for those who watch and observe from a distance. God strategically places people in our lives to observe our journey and learn life lessons at our expense. What we interpret as mistakes, others see as lessons of exposure and growth. Thank God for those who have endured moments of pain, grief, and failure to empower my life and enable me to become more successful at their cost.

Can I take a moment and be very transparent? The more I study the work of ministry, the more I become aware of the effort that many people put into covering up their limp. People work very diligently to make sure they appear to walk with great pride and purpose to ensure that people think they are perfect. Let me state a fact -no one is perfect, and no one believes that you are perfect. We all come short daily. It takes work and much effort to live a life of perpetrating perfection. It is easier to live genuinely attempting to please God, accept when we fall short, display the privilege of grace to allow God to correct us, and be truthful about our limps. The limp displays the reality of grace and the presence of God's glory. When you honestly stop to think about the fact that despite everything, you walk in success, it is evident that it was simply the grace of God. Everything we are and have become is simply by grace. The limp is evidence of grace. The limp is the vehicle God uses to remind us we did not get here alone without divine intervention. The limp is the daily reminder that not only have we survived by the grace of God, but the ability to continue operating requires grace's daily intervention. A leader without a limp is a leader that has not fully pursued their destiny. The limp becomes the evidence that God has sustained us and kept us as we endeavored to pursue vision and our God-given assignment. Never allow the difficulty of the limp to prevent you from continuing to pursue, learning to appreciate the limp, and not being discouraged by the reality of the limp.

Limit

When I was relatively young in ministry, I had the opportunity to pursue a serious evangelical season that would have put me on the road most days of the month. The proverbial carrot that was dangled in my face was the compensation. At the time, I was bi-vocational, and the ministry was not providing enough income to support my family. I almost fell into the trap of pursuing success based on compensation. The lessons learned in this season have been a guiding force for my decision-making throughout my career. Anyone that has not set limits (boundaries) in life will inevitably not achieve their full potential and impact on the world that God intended. I discovered the importance of setting boundaries (limits) in life. I remember a particular year when our church did not grow at all. That was the year that I also preached over 20 revivals. I stepped to God with a sacred attitude because it appeared that other churches were growing, and He had forgotten about our church. God spoke clearly to me that our church had not grown because the pastor (me) was unfocused

God would not send sheep without a shepherd.

and undisciplined. His exact response was that the church did not have a pastor but an evangelist. You see, God would not send sheep without a shepherd. I know many people will disagree with me, but I recognize the evangelist and the pastor as two distinctly different calls in the body of Christ. While the pastor must have an evangelist identity, the primary responsibility is shepherding sheep. There is a reason why Joyce Meyers does not pastor; she is an evangelist, not a shepherd. Once I clearly learned this lesson, I adjusted my lifestyle and established limits that shaped my God-given assignment. Have you noticed churches with a leader who spends a great amount of time on the road don't grow at the pace they are capable of growing? It's because staff management goes lacking, and spiritual development is limited. The old proverb is true; you can be a jack of all trades and master of none.

When I become clear on my assignment and establish boundaries based upon that assignment, it creates an atmosphere of consistency. I made a definitive decision only to pursue my primary assignment and created mental restrictions that developed consistency. I decided I wanted to be one of the most impactful pastors in my region. I was determined to succeed at pastoring where God had assigned me. John Kennedy once said anyone successful at anything has determined what they are willing to fail at. I am determined to fail at being well known around the world but succeeding at being impactful in my community. In ministry circles, I am an anomaly as I have only pastored one church, and I am not the founder. Mount Lebanon church is 100 years old. I firmly believe that my consistency has been the greatest gift to everyone connected to our church fellowship. Without established boundaries, we fall victim to allowing life and people to mandate our movements and convictions. When limits are established, they inform our decisions and create a mental culture of accountability. It becomes easier to say no when boundaries are created, maintained, and valued. Boundaries operate like officials in a sporting event; they define and enforce the rules of engagement. A person with reinforced boundaries will typically become more focused and have a clearer understanding of their God-given call and assignment.

In fact, you will never reach your full potential pursuing that which you have not been anointed to accomplish.

Have you ever noticed that people can articulate your call much clearer than they can their own? It appears that everyone knows what you should be doing, but no one knows what God has called them to do. My mother used to say some people were sent, and some people just went. Countless individuals have pursued calls and assignments because of a bogus word of prophecy from a relative and friend. It is dangerous to pursue assignments that have not been confirmed and reaffirmed by God. In fact, you will never reach your full potential pursuing that which you have not been anointed to accomplish. The anointing of God is His stamp of approval that we are in pursuit of the destiny He has called us to. I cringe when I hear people say, "they always told me I would preach." While I acknowledge that God uses

God's words are too powerful to waste.

people to speak words of clarification as we progress and mature in our spiritual walk, these affirmations should not be the sole source of confirmation. The voice of God should be the fullest confirmation that we are pursuing that which God intended for us to pursue. God desires to hold us accountable for being obedient to his commands and the purpose of life that He calls us to. I know what you are thinking; how do I know it is God? I hope this example helps. When I was a little boy, my mom would watch from inside the house if I was outside playing. As long as I was not doing something she did not agree with, she was fine. The moment I picked up rocks and began to throw them, she would knock on the window and shout, "put those rocks down before you break a window." As an adult, I have learned that people mistake how God speaks many times. Perhaps God's silence is communication. Rather than always being super spiritual and wanting God to speak audibly, appreciate His silence. When I began to pursue an assignment, if I am pleasing God, silence might be an affirmation. When I am pursuing that which is contrary to the will of God, He will speak. The body of Christ has fallen victim to spiritual gymnastics that make people feel inadequate to understand and comprehend the voice of God. Jesus was on the earth for 33 years, yet we have only a few times in scripture that God is speaking to him. Stop allowing people who testify about

God telling them what color dress to wear daily to make you feel God is not listening and observing your journey. God's words are too powerful to waste. God's words formed the universe. Maybe the silence of God is the confirmation you need to understand that God is, in fact, speaking.

Boundaries can assist in not allowing the voice of people to become louder and more definitive than the voice of God. People did not call you. People did not anoint you, and people cannot sustain the call of God on your life. Any successful person has also established relationship boundaries. My wife Valerie taught me to place people in several boxes. The boxes are colleagues, friends, acquaintances, family, and enemies. As you establish relationship boundaries, remember several things. First, you don't put people in boxes; they put themselves in boxes and believe them when they show you which box they belong in. Each box has a different level of relationship responsibility and obligation. As well, be open to acknowledging when you have people in the wrong box and move them accordingly. You don't have to inform anyone which box they are in. Your box is a mental record that you establish and operate your relationships by. Don't take it personally when you find out you had someone in the wrong box, make the adjustment and pursue success.

Lead

———..

Not long ago, I sat in a meeting led by Bishop T.D. Jakes. He began the conversation that morning with this statement; "I want to die empty." Those five words left a lasting impact on my thinking and, ultimately, my decision-making pertaining to leading. I had to ask myself, "what would be my eternal contribution to my family, my village, and the world?" Growing up, I would hear older people declare that "paying taxes and dying" were two things everyone had to do. One of the saddest realities is to die and not have known or fulfilled your assignment on earth. The second saddest reality is dying and not having deposited all that life has taught you into someone else. When the apostle Paul declares that he is ready to die, it is not a personal declaration of material success or personal accomplishment; it is a statement that he has left a legacy of wisdom and education in others. Paul further declares that my life has been poured out like a drink offering; in short, he is empty. To go to the grave and not have left an eternal deposit in the earth is the greatest waste of God-given potential. Leadership is not simply about people following you, but it is more about leading and discipling people. Furthermore, it's about depositing all that God has given you into others.

Every lesson learned becomes a generational vehicle to inform the next generation. One of the greatest gifts from people is the gift of being called their leader. Nothing is more powerful than watching people who have designated you as their leader beginning to walk out what you have taught by example and word. The greatest responsibility of a leader is the making of followers into teachers and examples. Every successful person has to ask constantly, what am I responsible for leaving as a leadership legacy? Success is not measured by simply leaving a financial inheritance but by knowledge, relationship, and critical thinking inheritance.

All behavior has the potential to have an educational impact. I have learned that most of us have disciples that we have never met. Please don't limit your intellectual deposit to only those in your bloodline. While it is vitally important for the success of a family legacy to make sure the next generation is taught, we should never forget that someone is observing everything we do. While there are many people who society has defined as being successful, I have learned that the most successful people have an internal desire to develop successful people.

I don't want my success measured by material possessions, academic credentials, or personal positions when I die. I want people to look at my children and see the qualities of life that I modeled. Can you imagine living your life as a model of consistency to the extent that your great-grandchildren walk out your convictions and behavior? The pursuit of success is grounded in the desire to see those you lead go further than you did. There are days that I sit and dream about what my grandchildren and great-grandchildren will accomplish. Leave no excuses for the next generation. Make it hard for them to fail. I often hear my wife tell our children that if they don't do well in life, it will not be because we did not leave them positioned for success. Again, that positioning must include more than just finances.

Perhaps the greatest blessing of successful leadership is the prevention of repeated lessons. Life is a university that teaches many lessons. Some of the lessons of life are painful and difficult to learn. No education is free; the price of those lessons is the instruction of the next generation. Why would anyone want their disciples to have to repeat the lessons they have learned? Leading people is about giving them the ability to progress faster because they don't have to waste time and opportunities in the classroom of life. Disciples should always grow at a rate faster than their leader. My children should go much further than me. They should have a greater impact and achieve much more. It is, in fact, a principle that Jesus modeled. He told His disciples that they would do more than He had. His exact words were, "greater thing than I did, you shall do" John 14:2. Why? Because he had positioned them to progress faster. The burden of the leader is to be transparent before his disciples. Jesus allowed his disciples to see him weep, wrestle with decisions in the garden and forgive those who had mistreated him. After over three decades of ministry, one thing that has been made very clear is how hard it is for many leaders to display transparency. Tell the next generation how you got to where you are. Don't sugarcoat the journey with hyperbole. When dealing with tough subjects such as sexuality, decision-making, and relationships, be honest and open. It is extremely empowering to let people see the real you. To understand that you are not some super Christian. Too many people stop pursuing their dreams and potential because they feel inadequate or disqualified because of decisions that led to mistakes. Allowing people to see how we have survived moments that the adversary designed to derail our future creates an atmosphere of redemption for those who are followers. Again, too often, children feel an unhealthy pressure to live up to their parents' standards because their parents have not allowed them to see the parts of life that display the grace of God.

I am convinced that any successful person has achieved that success by the grace of God. While there is the reality of personal effort, conviction, and perseverance, the absence of God's grace limits the level of success. God repeatedly looks beyond our faults and still sees our needs. Allowing your children to identify those moments where the grace of God intervened in your journey is inspirational. All success is driven by the concept of a village. While the village might not always be as identifiable for everyone, all of us are the product of learning from a leader. Successful people don't teach only positive lessons, but they also teach what not to do.

Pursuing success for only personal gain is such a selfish posture of living. Instead, we should pursue success for the implications of legacy. Remember, when the tide comes in, all boats rise. I want my bloodline successful, my village successful, and my church family successful. Finally, pursuing success allows me to give and create the definition of success. I never wanted the world-defining success for my family and me and our ministry. I wanted to give the world my definition of success. My desire is not to meet the world's standard but to develop a God-centered standard and inspire the world to adopt my definition and standard of success. I want to stand up and announce to the world and the adversary you better watch out because I am raising a generation of world changers who will pursue Godly success and ultimately bring glory to the Kingdom of God.

I want to create pastures...

Amazed by His Grace,
Bishop Kim W. Brown